ENDOR

The writer of Ecclesiastes said, "A threefold cord is not easily broken." Most spirit-filled believers have received "the anointing." Some, like Elisha, received a double portion. This young generation needs a *Triple Threat Anointing*—an unlimited flow to break the yokes of satan (see Isa. 10:27).

The *Triple Threat Anointing* impacts man's tri-part nature, which is made up of the body, soul, and spirit. It flows within three realms—heaven, earth, and the underworld. It moves from Heaven to earth and shakes the foundations of hell!

I have known Andrew Towe since he was a child. He has loved the Lord from an early age and has matured into a powerful Word-centered minister. He has been connected to anointed vessels his entire life. He understands the ebb and flow of the anointing that creates a three-fold cord of power to set a person free indeed!

Do not just read this book. Act upon it and set a generation free!

PERRY STONE, JR.
International evangelist and Bible teacher
Best-selling author of *Secrets of the Third Heaven* and
The Danger of Fishing in the Sea of Forgetfulness
Host of *Manna-Fest with Perry Stone*

In this amazing book, *The Triple Threat Anointing*, the Lord has sent a message of *hope* to *all* who believe! In a world of confusion and darkness, He is coming with unstoppable power, just as He promised. As you read this prophetic declaration, you will be given biblical strategies that will increase your faith and bring the miraculous into your life, your family, and your world. Andrew Towe is a man sent from God with a word from Heaven...get ready to be changed by it!

KAREN WHEATON
Recording artist and preacher
Author of *Watching the Road*
Founder and host of *The Ramp with Karen Wheaton*

Wow, wow, wow! *The Triple Threat Anointing* by my friend Pastor Andrew Towe is one of the most powerful books and prophetic revelations to hit the world; it is definitely for *right now*. Get your hands on it, your eyes in it, and watch God ignite your heart for the next supernatural outpouring. A must-read!

JUDY JACOBS
Bible teacher and recording artist
Author of *Take It by Force, You Are Anointed for This*, and *Stand Strong*

The greatest attacks on your life by the enemy always precede the most powerful outpourings of the Holy Spirit. Andrew Towe's *The Triple Threat Anointing* is the ultimate prophetic manual and revelation for what God has promised, prepared, and is sending to your life—*epic!*

JAMIE TUTTLE
Lead pastor, Dwelling Place Church
Cleveland, Tennessee

In every generation God places His hand on a man, and within the man He forges a message. Thus a messenger, with a unique voice that can be heard, emerges. Andrew Towe is a relevant prophetic, evangelistic, and apostolic voice who carries just what this potent book entails—a *triple threat!* This powerful book declassifies the secrets of God as it pertains to the coming supernatural movement of His Spirit. I believe this book is a right-now prophetic word for the Body of Christ for this new era. *The Triple Threat Anointing* is not a book for chocolate soldiers ready to melt under heated pressure due to spiritual warfare. But will rise up with a *Triple Threat Anointing* of the Holy Spirit to advance the kingdom of God. This prophetic book is the prelude and interpretation of Andrew's dream of the prophecy spoken by Joel the prophet, which is echoed by Peter (see Acts 2:14-21).

Furthermore, "From the days of John the Baptist until now," there has been an extraordinary rush of people pressing in from all sides, eager for a blessing. The "kingdom of heaven suffers violence," figuratively speaking, in that people were so thronging to hear the gospel that they resembled an army trying to besiege a city. And the "violent take it by force"—the people entering the kingdom were not violent literally, but their eagerness to see the coming of the Messiah was so overwhelming that it was as if they were attacking a city and beating down the doors to enter. Are you ready to relentlessly take the kingdom by force in this new move of God? *The Triple Threat Anointing* is your new marching orders to become a "triple threat" against the unseen enemies of God's Spirit movement in this third-day awakening!

DR. HAKEEM COLLINS
Prophetic voice and international speaker
Author of *Heaven Declares, Prophetic Breakthrough, Command Your Healing,*
and *101 Prophetic Ways God Speaks*

The book you hold in your hands, *The Triple Threat Anointing*, is a must-read for anyone looking to move deeper into the supernatural life. Andrew Towe's book shares amazing principles and testimonies of the reality of the ascended life that give us understanding and empowerment into kingdom dynamics. *The Triple Threat Anointing* will leave you hungering for more of God and equip you to stand strong in the power of the Gospel of Jesus the Messiah.

PROPHET JEFF JANSEN
Global Fire Ministries International
Senior leader, Global Fire Church
Author of *Glory Rising, Furious Sound of Glory*
Host, *Decoding the Supernatural,* ISN Network

Andrew Towe is a tremendous apostolic and prophetic voice to the Body of Christ. Valora and I have known Andrew for years and we have ministered together on many platforms. Our churches have always been blessed by the insight and wisdom he releases each time he ministers. His revelation concerning the *Triple Threat Anointing* is guaranteed to unlock and catapult many believers into the next level of their purpose and destiny. The understanding that the next era of the church will be ushered in through those who both receive and release salvation, healing, and deliverance is tremendous. It is our belief that every believer should have this resource in their arsenal of tools and allow it to become ingrained in their spirit. Allow the words that you read in this book to activate the *Triple Threat Anointing* on your life so that you can be used by God to usher in a harvest of souls through salvation, healing, and deliverance.

LaJun and Valora Cole
Authors of *Sudden Breakthrough* and
The Power of a Fearless Voice
Founders, LaJun and Valora Cole Ministries
Lead servants, Contagious Churches

I could not put the book down! A fire has been lit inside of me since reading *The Triple Threat Anointing*. In fact, from the very first chapter when I read about the dream that Prophet Andrew Towe had regarding this *triple threat anointing* where Jesus appeared to him, I've been determined to be a part of this next great movement of God which Pastor Towe so beautifully describes and foretells. I guarantee you that as you read this book a deep hunger for more of Jesus will envelop you even as it has me.

CAROL ELAINE, TH.D.
President and founder of Carol Elaine
Ministries, ¡WOW! (Women of the Word), and
co-founder of Christ Exalted Seminary
Author of *God Bless This Home* and
Mantles of the Daughter
Hostess of the television show *Contact*
Station Manager CTN Vegas in Las Vegas, NV

I love how God chooses to mark people with unique messages for coming movements and, as they release them, become the catalyst for that very outpouring in the earth. I believe Andrew Towe is one of those people who God has branded with a message to the church and that message is that we are stepping into a new mantle and new anointing for this new era we are in, to see Jesus magnified in the earth! If you have felt powerless and disillusioned in your walk and confused about your purpose, then this book is for you. It's a feast to be devoured and strength to cause you to stand to your feet for this exciting time of history we are in.

NATE and CHRISTY JOHNSTON
Founders of Everyday Revivalists

THE
TRIPLE
THREAT
ANOINTING

THE
TRIPLE
THREAT
ANOINTING

Moving in the Supernatural Power of
SALVATION, HEALING, & DELIVERANCE

ANDREW TOWE

DEDICATION

I dedicate this book to my best friend, Jesus. Every breath that I breathe, every word that I speak and everything that I will ever do, is all for You. My life's theme scripture was written in a letter from the Apostle Paul when he was locked in a Roman jail as a political prisoner. This verse is etched in every beat of my heart and serves as a constant reminder of my purpose.

> *Therefore I, a prisoner for serving the Lord, beg you to lead a life worthy of your calling, for you have been called by God* (Ephesians 4:1 NLT).

My desire is that I will be able to live my life worthy of my calling. My prayer is that Your heart's desire for this Triple Threat Movement will come soon and You will flow through all of us to accomplish Your purpose for this generation.

DESTINY IMAGE® PUBLISHERS, INC.

P.O. Box 310, Shippensburg, PA 17257-0310

"Promoting Inspired Lives."

This book and all other Destiny Image and Destiny Image Fiction books are available at Christian bookstores and distributors worldwide.

Cover design by Eileen Rockwell

Interior design by Terry Clifton

For more information on foreign distributors, call 717-532-3040.

Reach us on the Internet: www.destinyimage.com.

ISBN 13 TP: 978-0-7684-5714-8

ISBN 13 eBook: 978-0-7684-5715-5

ISBN 13 HC: 978-0-7684-5717-9

ISBN 13 LP: 978-0-7684-5716-2

For Worldwide Distribution, Printed in the U.S.A.

1 2 3 4 5 6 7 8 / 24 23 22 21 20

CONTENTS

FOREWORD

Some time ago, my spiritual son, Andrew Towe, shared his prophetic word concerning the triple threat with me. I was taken aback by the language and scope of the word. I endeavor to remain in a position of leaning in and listening to God's prophets concerning the times and seasons.

I made up my mind a long time ago that I want to be on the cutting edge of the move of God. I don't want to be stale. I want to be flowing in the new wine and the latest thing that God is doing in the earth. I know the religious get angry about the idea of God doing anything new, but let's remember that He is constantly leading us to discover new levels of His goodness and mercy. As prophetic people, we can live tuned in. We can remain in a posture of seeking and serving.

> *Believe in the Lord your God, so shall ye be established; believe his prophets, so shall ye prosper* (2 Chronicles 20:20).

The word *prosper* here is an interesting word. In Hebrew, one of the meanings is to break out. I believe that the prophetic anointing causes people to break out. They break forth from stagnation, complacency, and lethargy. They also break free from bondage and restriction. There is power in the revelation of the mind of God.

When the prophetic anointing is released, it will tear down longstanding walls. It will clear the path of debris and rubble. It will break people out of tradition void of the life of God. This is why prophets, prophetic worship, and prophetic ministry are vital to the move of God. We need to be in sync with what God is saying and doing in the earth.

God uses prophets to bring us up to speed. I believe God is raising up prophetic mouthpieces to give language to the moves He is birthing in the earth. I use the word *moves* instead of *move* because I believe it is global and it is diverse.

I do not believe that God is going to limit Himself to one style, one flow, or one expression. I believe He is breaking forth on every front in tsunami fashion. We must learn to discern the next set of spiritual waves, jump on them, and ride. This is the way that I believe God is moving in this hour. There is no time for fear. Fear will limit your ability to move in the next thing God is doing. Fear paralyzes you, but faith releases you. Faith causes you to move into the unknown.

We are often going into the unknown, moving into unfamiliar territory. We are speaking mysteries that God has unraveled to us. We are pioneering new wineskin ministries for which we have no manual! We have to keep a bent knee and an open heart. This is the strategy to engage the next move.

The language in this book is prophetic. Andrew speaks as a prophet, unfolding the mysteries of Heaven. He speaks of a coming move! Let this book stir your faith! Let this book provoke hunger in your spirit!

Do not pick this book up if you are not daring, if you just want to be a mediocre Christian. This book is dangerous! It will knock you out of complacency and cause you to press. I was so stirred when I first heard this word because I had already seen in a vision part of what is described in these pages. I believe there is a move at hand that will help bring in the harvest of the nations. It is not a normal move of God. It is a *triple threat!*

RYAN LESTRANGE
Author *Sixty Days of Unusual*
Founder TRIBE, iHubs, RLM

CHAPTER 1

_____•○•_____

WHAT IS THE TRIPLE THREAT ANOINTING?

‖ THE VISION OF A MOVEMENT ‖

The Lord spoke to me concerning a new move of God that is coming. He said, *"I am uprooting religious systems and tearing down man's ways of doing things. This new move will be marked by My glory and the flow will be pure."*

I had been preaching a series of messages on a new move of God for several months at my church in Chattanooga, Tennessee. In May of 2019, I had a dream unlike any that I have ever had. God showed me a divine revelation of the coming move of God and what we're going to see occur in this great awakening. As soon as I had the dream, I began to prophesy about the coming move of God.

In my dream, the Lord took me to stadiums that were filled to capacity. Jesus and I were standing in the concession area at the top of the stadium, looking down at what was playing out before our eyes. He instructed me, saying, *"Watch what is about to take place."* I looked in the direction to which He drew my attention and saw people running to the altars to give their lives to Jesus. And it wasn't just hundreds of people that I saw aggressively hurrying to the altars. I saw masses responding to His salvation call. What captivated me was they didn't take their time, politely meandering up to the front. I could see a hunger and desperation for Him in each one of them, unlike anything I have ever seen in my lifetime. It was clear to me that He allowed me to view the scene not only in what appeared to be the physical realm, but also in the supernatural realm. I could visibly see the people being transformed from darkness to light in a moment. This change that was occurring in them was not because of their emotions but a supernatural encounter with the glory of God.

What happened next was beyond anything words can describe. I witnessed a mighty wave of healing sweep over the multitudes. Even now I do not have words to describe the enormity of the droves of people who received healing or the greatness of those who were healed by the miracle-working power of God as His Spirit moved among the people, transforming their bodies and souls. I get emotional now just thinking about it.

As I stood there with my mouth opened in utter amazement, Jesus then said to me, *"Look again."* I turned to see what He wanted me to see. I saw among the great myriad of people those captive and the tormented, I was astounded at their great number. I watched in terror due to their awful suffering and agony. They were in horrific bondage. Heavy chains draped around them and the weight of those chains seemed almost unbearable. My heart ached for them as I watched many of them trying with all their might to worship the Lord. The harder they strained to worship Jesus, the more restricted they became, even to the point they could no longer move. I saw the reason for their immobility. Each time they tried to lift their hands to the Lord, demonic forces would come and pull on those heavy chains, causing the captive and the tormented to become even more restricted. As they tried to lift their voice to worship, the evil spirits would muzzle their mouths. *Jesus, please help them,* I thought to myself. And suddenly, the glory and the mercy of God fell! I saw mass deliverances taking place among the captives and the tormented. God's power set them totally free. Simultaneously, the heavy chains instantly broke off, the demonic spirits vanished, and the people who filled the stadium began to worship the Lord. The whole stadium seemed to have become one choir; their worship was the most beautiful sound that I had ever heard. They flowed together in such harmony, as if they had been collectively rehearsing it for years. Their worship filled the atmosphere, and the Lord Jesus Christ received all their worship. It was an intoxicating atmosphere.

I was overwhelmed that all of this was taking place in one gathering. Most of the stadium services that I have ever attended were heavily focused on either salvation, healing, or deliverance, but in this one all three were occurring. I turned to the Lord and said, "I have never seen anything like this." With great excitement and almost what I would deem giddiness, He said to me, "*I know. It is a Triple Threat Movement!*" It was as though He had been anxiously waiting for this moment to move in such a way.

Later, reflecting on the dream, I was puzzled over the name He gave the move—*triple threat*. I was accustomed to the term being used in the entertainment industry, describing an entertainer who could sing, dance, and act, but to be used in the move of God baffled me. It was then the Lord reminded me of the spiritual significance of the number three. The Temple was separated into three parts—the outer court, the inner court, and the Holy of Holies. In Scripture, it is the picture of wholeness or completeness, as well as being the number of resurrection. Three is the number of God—Father, Son, and the Holy Spirit.

God also used the number three to announce another great movement that was recorded in Acts 10 when Peter went into a trance and saw Heaven opened:

*But he became hungry and wanted something to eat. While the meal was being prepared he fell into a trance; and he saw the sky opened up, and an object like a great sheet descending, lowered by its four corners to the earth, and it contained all kinds of four-footed animals and crawling creatures of the earth and birds of the air. A voice came to him, "Get up, Peter, kill and eat!" But Peter said, "Not at all, Lord, for I have never eaten anything that is common (unholy) and [ceremonially] unclean." And the voice came to him a second time, "What God has cleansed and pronounced clean, no longer consider common (unholy)." This happened **three times**, and then immediately the object was taken up into heaven* (Acts 10:10-16 AMP).

Peter's vision was an illustration that God desired to bring salvation to both the Jews and Gentiles. He confirmed this to Peter by the great sheet descending three times. In essence, God was instructing to Peter to preach the message of the Gospel to everyone. The vision was a prophetic announcement that God was releasing a movement that would shake the world.

I believe the Lord showed me this Triple Threat Movement as a prophetic announcement that there is a day fast approaching that God will move upon this earth, using ordinary people who have been equipped with the

Triple Threat Anointing. We will see an army that not only carries God's glory inside of them but will release His glory through them. These warriors will see God pouring out the oil of salvation, healing, and deliverance! Furthermore, the Holy Spirit spoke to me, saying, *"In this Triple the enemy's tactics will be exposed and the Threat will be God's people arising to the forefront."* God's glorious Church will rise up in power and take dominion over the enemy. The hour is upon us to take new ground and put the devil on the run.

Let's take another look at the number three:

> *Go through the camp and tell the people to get their provisions ready. In three days you will cross the Jordan River and take possession of the land the Lord your God is giving you* (Joshua 1:11 NLT).

God ordered Joshua on the *"third day"* to cross the Jordan and to take possession of territory that God had given them. The Triple Threat will be a "third day" resurrection for the Body of Christ. The Church will experience long-dead promises being resurrected and possessing of territory that God has given the Church. Dead religion is not our portion but rather possessing the territories that God has called us to inherit as joint heirs with Christ.

> *Only ask, and I will give you the nations as your inheritance, the whole earth as your possession* (Psalm 2:8 NLT).

The Triple Threat Movement that I saw was especially unique and unlike any previous outpourings or revivals. It was not just one, two, or even three particular ministers who were featured on the platform. I saw ministry teams each using their gifts that released the strong flow. There is an army arising that will function much like that of the early Church.

> *Now there are diversities of gifts, but the same Spirit. And there are differences of administrations, but the same Lord. And there are diversities of operations, but it is the same God which worketh all in all* (1 Corinthians 12:4-6).

The alarm is sounding and the bride of Christ is rousing from her slumber. The call of awakening has gone forth. I believe that we are crossing the threshold and into this *Triple Threat Anointing* that will birth the movement that I was shown. Can you hear the call to come deeper with Him? Do you feel the tug of the Spirit? The Holy Spirit is declaring to you, *"There is more."* Will you respond to the call of the Spirit to move into the deep?

> *Deep calls unto deep at the noise of Your waterfalls; all Your waves and billows have gone over me* (Psalm 42:7 NKJV).

The prophet Joel prophesied about such an outpouring.

And it shall come to pass afterward that I will pour out My Spirit on all flesh; your sons and your daughters shall prophesy, your old men shall dream dreams, your young men shall see visions. And also on My menservants and on My maidservants I will pour out My Spirit in those days (Joel 2:28-29 NKJV).

Joel clearly described the outpouring of God's Spirit upon all flesh, and Peter quoted him in the Book of Acts on the Day of Pentecost (see Acts 2:17-18). The 120 who had tarried experienced an outpouring and were baptized with the Holy Ghost fire. Everything changed in that moment. I believe that this generation will see another outpouring, a third great awakening that is going to take place. A *"this is that"* movement. It will be unexplainable, incomparable, but a genuine move of the Holy Spirit.

But Peter, standing up with the eleven, lifted up his voice, and said unto them, Ye men of Judaea, and all ye that dwell at Jerusalem, be this known unto you, and hearken to my words: For these are not drunken, as ye suppose, seeing it is but the third hour of the day. But this is that which was spoken by the prophet Joel; And it shall come to pass in the last days, saith God, I will pour out of my Spirit upon all flesh: and your sons and your daughters shall prophesy, and your young men shall see visions, and your old men shall dream dreams (Acts 2:14-17).

You might be looking at those Scriptures and saying to yourself, "Joel's prophecy was fulfilled and now I must settle for a brand of powerless, nice Christianity." I boldly declare to you, "*No!*" God desires to flow through you with the Holy Spirit's power. The Greek word for the power of the Holy Spirit is *dunamis,* and from it come the words *dynamo* and *dynamite.* This power cannot be contained or hidden. Dynamite is explosive. It is the time for you to move beyond proclaiming the power of the Holy Spirit and begin *demonstrating* His power. We are on the preface of believers awakening to and walking in their God-given authority given to us through the name of Jesus.

When Jesus appeared to John on the Greek island of Patmos, He revealed that He possesses the keys of authority over the enemy. He said to John, *"I am He who lives, and was dead, and behold, I am alive forevermore. Amen. And I have the keys of Hades and of Death"* (Rev. 1:18 NKJV). Keys are a symbol of authority. Keys have the assignment to give access to things that have been locked up. Jesus declared that He has the authority over death, satan, and all of hell.

Jesus came up and said to them, "All authority (all power of absolute rule) in heaven and on earth has been given to Me. Go therefore and make disciples of all the nations [help the people to learn of Me, believe in Me, and obey My words], baptizing them in the name of the Father and of the Son and of the Holy Spirit" (Matthew 28:18-19 AMP).

Furthermore, Jesus said the following:

And these miracle signs will accompany those who believe: They will drive out demons in the power of my name. They will speak in tongues. They will be supernaturally protected from snakes and from drinking anything poisonous. And they will lay hands on the sick and heal them (Mark 16:17-18 TPT).

Did you see that? The One who has the keys of authority decreed that those who believe in the power of His name will have *"miracle signs"* through the power of His name. Do you believe in His name? If the answer is yes, then know that He has delegated to you authority to use His name, the name of Jesus. You have been authorized to use His name against sin, sickness, and devils. There are those who have said, "All those things have passed away. Believers casting out devils is done away with. The gift of tongues is not available to the modern-day believer. Miracles and healings no longer happen. Our dependence for good health is regulated to only the doctors who practice medicine." Let me boldly say to you, *"No!* God is still the Deliverer, the Healer, and the Miracle Worker." I know firsthand because He has been those things to me. Let me share with you how I have experienced the power of the *Triple Threat Anointing* in my own life.

SALVATION AND DELIVERANCE

Jesus has been my Savior my entire life. I cannot remember a time when I did not serve the Lord and know Him as my Savior. I do not have a dramatic story connected with my salvation; however, I have found that walking with Jesus and staying planted in the knowledge of God is the greatest testimony anyone could ever have.

I went through a hellish depression for three years. I left my house very few times during that period. I had placed aluminum foil over the windows to block light from getting in. I unplugged all of my phones and refused to answer the door for anyone. I stopped eating and wasted away to 130 pounds, and for my height and frame it was a deathly low weight.

I have served the Lord my whole life and was filled with the Holy Ghost at the young age of four. I recorded albums, traveled, and sang all over the world for Jesus, yet I somehow found myself locked in the prison of depression. During that time, I could not hear God's voice. I just wanted to hear His voice, and honestly I didn't care if it was even in a rebuke. I would turn on Christian television and still felt like He was so far from me. I would go to my prayer room and try to pray as I have done my whole life, and it was as if my prayers did not go past the ceiling. I had never been in such a lonely place. I had always met with Him. Even as a small boy, I would give Him nightly concerts, and as I worshiped He always came. What had I done to separate us? Why did He not see what I was going through? I could not understand this place. I hated it. I now understand that I was in a test, much like when Job was tested and he couldn't hear God's voice. However, through it all, Job remained faithful.

> *Look, I go forward, but He is not there, and backward, but I cannot perceive Him; when He works on the left hand, I cannot behold Him; when He turns to the right hand, I cannot see Him. But He knows the way that I take; when He has tested me, I shall come forth as gold* (Job 23:8-10 NKJV).

After three years of constant battle, I was tired. I found myself at the end of my rope after three days of not sleeping, not eating, and not even showering, but only staring vacantly at a wall in my bedroom. *That's it. I can't take it anymore. The confusion, the torment, the anguish must end. I don't want to die, but I can't live another day in the prison of mental suffering.* I was unaware that this was the day that God had orchestrated my deliverance.

As I lay in my bed with tears streaming down my face, I began to think about what I could take in my medicine cabinet to bring an end to this battle. The enemy had me convinced that this world would be better without me. I just did not want to exist anymore. As my mind begin to play out the scenario of how this would stop the pain, *suddenly* something unexpected happened. I had Christian television playing in the background, as I did frequently during this time. One line of a song being sung hit my spirit. I could only describe it as a quickening. It felt as if a bolt of electricity had hit my spirit. I was surprised because it had been so long since I felt this kind of a stirring.

Immediately, I grabbed my Bible and went into my living room. I will never forget where I was standing and what happened to me that day. I raised my Bible in the air and with all the strength that I could muster, I released a cry of desperation. I said, "The God whom I have served my entire life, if You are really real, then I need for You to come and deliver me today. Help me." I want to tell you that the presence of God filled my little living room, and that day God set me free. I know Him as the Deliverer! The chains that were wrapped around me broke that day. He is still the chain breaker!

HEALING

I also know Him to be the Healer and Miracle Worker. I have so many testimonies of His healing power. However, in 2011 one week before our first baby, Giuliana Faith Towe, was to be born, out of nowhere I had a grand mal seizure. It happened as I lay in bed with my wife. We were talking one minute, and then all of a sudden I began seizing. She called 911 and an ambulance was sent to our house. I finally awakened out of the seizure and they took me to a local hospital. I continued having seizures throughout the next few days, while in the hospital. The doctors could not find what was causing them. They finally released me from the hospital to go home. I was scheduled for a follow-up appointment the next week with my neurologist. The next week was more than enough time to have the intercessors from our church, my family, and me pray and believe God for a miracle. My wife was extremely pregnant and very worried about me, as I was worried about her. We had lost several babies before, and I did not want her carrying the weight of this pressure on her.

My wife went with me to the follow-up appointment with one of the top neurologists in the Southeast. He said, "Mr. Towe, understand that you had seven ministrokes in your brain. You may never be able to regain all of your clear speech."

I replied, "I understand, that is what you say." I refused to come into agreement with the enemy's lie over me.

The doctor looked at me, almost with sympathy as if I were in denial. He said, "Come back here and let me show you on your MRI." We walked to the back of his practice, where there was a computer with a large monitor and two chairs that were pulled up to the counter. He sat in one, and I gave the other to my very pregnant wife. He pulled up my MRI. I was standing behind him, praying in the Holy Ghost the whole time. He looked at it for a second as though he were searching it out; then he said, "That is strange. This does not look like the MRI that I saw when you were in the hospital." By this time my spirit man was leaping inside me and I felt as though I could have taken off running and done a Jericho march right there in his practice. He then said, "Can you come back in an hour? I need to consult with some of the other doctors on this."

I said, "Of course. There's a Chick-fil-A downstairs." My wife Brooke and I ate good that day.

We went back after the hour was up and the doctor said to us, "After consulting with the other doctors, we have concluded that you never had a mini-stroke. Have you ever had a car accident?"

I said, "Yes, I have had two serious car accidents."

He continued, saying, "We have determined that the seizure was a result of blunt force trauma to your brain during a car accident. There was bleeding on the brain, but according to your MRI it has healed nicely and the seizures were an electrical current that occurred as a result. You will need to take medication to keep you from having any more seizures, but other than that you are good to go."

Did you get that? The doctor said that I had *"never had a mini-stroke."* You serve a God who can change the findings of an MRI. I don't believe that the findings were a mistake. I believe that was my God's miracle-working power. I know Him to be the Healer!

God desires that you not only experience the power of the Holy Spirit through the *Triple Threat Anointing* in your life, but He wants you to operate in this anointing. He longs for this anointing to flow through you to impact those around you. Are you willing to be a vessel for the Master's use?

This new move of God will be as a tsunami. It will be unstoppable. The days of relegating the Holy Spirit to the back room are over! His gifts are making a comeback in the Church. This move cannot be manufactured. It is fueled by a radical pursuit of Jesus. Get ready for God's *Triple Threat* to be released through believers and change the world!

This is your divine invitation to enter into this anointing. Will you answer the call?

CHAPTER 2

———•○•———

MARKED BY GLORY

‖ FOR GREAT EXPLOITS ‖

This new move of God is going to be marked (set apart) by glory. The children of God will encounter His glory in a new way and these encounters will empower them to do great exploits. There are no limitations in the glory of God. The impossible is suddenly possible. The supernatural is unexplainably natural. We must move into the glory realm to accomplish the plan of God for this generation.

One of my favorite examples in the Word of God of an individual whom God marked by His glory and used to do great exploits is Moses. Moses was destined to be a deliverer. His name means "drew out." Not only was he drawn out of the waters of the Nile River—his mother had placed him in a basket to protect him from the decree of Pharaoh to kill all the male babies—later, he was used to draw all the Israelites out of the Red Sea.

Moses was adopted by the daughter of Pharaoh and raised in the palace. He was provided with the best education and had access to the finest of things. Nonetheless, Moses was marked by God for a great purpose. Even though he could have rested in his royal position and enjoyed life's comforts, there was a mandate constantly pulling for him to fulfill.

Moses saw firsthand the injustice that was dealt to his people, the Israelites, from the Egyptians. There was an ever-present conflict inside of him. He must have felt as if he was in a tug-of-war match. Staying loyal to his royal adopted family on one end and making a stand for his enslaved people on the other. After witnessing an Egyptian killing one of his Hebrew brethren along with the continued abuse and mistreatment of them, he could take no more. He rose up and killed the Egyptian murderer and hid him in the sand. Here is where we see Moses doing a right thing but at the wrong time. He was attempting to deliver the Hebrews but by his own might and not by the Lord's direction.

The next day he tried to intervene with two Hebrews who were fighting. The Hebrew men then asked him if he would kill them the way that he killed the Egyptian. Fear and panic gripped his heart. Thoughts of "Surely everyone knows what I did" plagued his mind. When this information got to the ears of Pharaoh, he was furious and sought to kill Moses. In the natural way of thinking, we would conclude that this was the end of Moses. He blew it. His story was now over. However, he was purposed to be God's deliverer. I am so thankful that God does not throw people away whenever we blow it.

God was with Moses and led him to an isolated place for God to prepare him for his destiny. Some of you reading this have felt the pain of isolation. I declare to you today that you are being prepared for your greatest hour. It is not *over* for you just like it was not over for Moses!

> *Now Moses kept the flock of Jethro his father in law, the priest of Midian: and he led the flock to the backside of the desert, and came to the mountain of God, even to Horeb. And the angel of the Lord appeared unto him in a flame of fire out of the midst of a bush: and he looked, and, behold, the bush burned with fire, and the bush was not consumed. And Moses said, I will now turn aside, and see this great sight, why the bush is not burnt. And when the Lord saw that he turned aside to see, God called unto him out of the midst of the bush, and said, Moses, Moses. And he said, Here am I (Exodus 3:1-4).*

Moses was on the run, isolated in hiding, leading his father-in-law's sheep to the backside of the desert when out of nowhere he had an encounter with the glory of God. His preparation had finally aligned with God's divine plan. Moses' seemingly normal life was interrupted by the glory. This encounter would forever shift his life and finally move him into his purpose.

Does God have permission to interrupt your life? Or do you already have a five-year plan where everything is laid out and your desire is for God to move within the confines of the structure you have built? God has a way of shaking the foundations of our plans and desires to bring about His purpose.

I have served the Lord for as long as I can remember. I was active in ministry since I was a small child. I began singing in my local church, and then, at the ripe old age of eight, I recorded my first gospel album. The next several years I continued to sing and was able to record more albums. I sang at various churches, camp meetings, and seminars. Wherever anyone would invite me to minister, I would be there with a song ready to go. It did not matter to me if it was two people or thousands; I loved to tell people about Jesus. When I was seventeen, I finally had funding to be able to record in Nashville with the Grammy award-winning producer Lari Goss. He produced albums for many of my favorite gospel singers. In my opinion, his masterful orchestrations could not be matched by anyone. I felt that God had finally opened the door that was going to take my ministry to the next level.

Up until this point, my previous recordings had been low-budget, locally produced recordings. I was very careful selecting the songs for this album. I ministered each song live numerous times before going into the studio to lay down the tracks for them. Doing so gives you a better idea of what flows and what doesn't flow. I wanted to make sure that these songs gripped people's hearts and made a lasting impact on their lives. I finally found the ten songs that I believed were the perfect fit. We recorded the project with some of the best-known studio musicians. It was a dream come true. I loved every minute of it.

I believed this album would cause doors to swing open all over the world. However, that was not the case. I could not believe that I had a great album, with powerful songs and amazing arrangements, but no one was hearing it. My hope turned to disappointment.

> *Hope deferred makes the heart sick: but when the desire comes, it is a tree of life* (Proverbs 13:12 NKJV).

I came to the decision that ministry was not for me. I had been ministering to people since I was a small boy, but now I was going to focus entirely on me. I reasoned that I could still be a Christian and serve God, but not hold the responsibility of ministry. I decided that I was going to college to earn a degree in graphic design, open my own business, and make a lot of money. I would give finances and fund the kingdom of God. This would satisfy the longing of ministry and telling people about Jesus.

I remember slipping in late to my local church where I previously served as worship leader. I sat on the back row. I did not want anyone to notice me. I didn't want anyone to ask me to pray for them or sing a song. I just kept saying to myself that I just wanted to be normal. I convinced myself that I had tried the ministry thing, willing to do anything and go anywhere to tell people about Jesus, but now it was time for something new. I even said, "There's nothing wrong with normal and being a back-row Christian." I would enjoy being comfortable, having no pressure or responsibility, and not always having to be an example—just normal.

However, God had set me aside before I was formed in my mother's belly. When God has set you aside, He will cause you not to fit in the places you try to wedge yourself in. Like a misplaced puzzle piece, even though you try to jam it in, it just doesn't work. God will cause you not to fit so that you will seek Him and He can fulfill His purpose in your life. He took my "yes" seriously when I started nightly prayer meetings in my bedroom, when I would give Him a concert for One. Singing at the top of my lungs and with tears streaming down my face, I would say, "God, I will do anything for You. Please use me." There was nothing "ordinary" about that. My heavenly Father had made a deposit in me that He would not allow to go to waste.

I tried my best to fit in the confines of "normal," but the more I tried, the more I stood out. I did not do what other "normal" kids, even Christian kids, were doing. I had been marked by God. There were times I would cry out in frustration to Him, "Why won't You just let me be normal?" The calling of God was ever present with me. I could not shake it. There was no escaping it. He would speak to me in my dreams. Almost every service I went to, no matter how I tried to hide and not make eye contact with the minister, I would be called out and given a prophetic word. God was loudly proclaiming to me, "You are not normal. You are set apart. You have been marked by My glory." I know firsthand what Moses experienced. I tried to launch out with music ministry, but it didn't work the way I planned. Moses tried to intervene and be a deliverer to the Hebrews in his own power. It didn't work out too good for him when he ended up killing a man and hiding him in the sand.

For the span of forty years, Moses was satisfied in the desert. He was living the desert dream. He had the wife, the family, the white picket fence, but everything was about to change. One day out of nowhere, bam! The angel of the Lord appeared:

> *And the angel of the Lord appeared unto him in a flame of fire out of the midst of a bush: and he looked, and, behold, the bush burned with fire, and the bush was not consumed* (Exodus 3:2).

The "angel of the Lord" here is one of the Trinity, most likely Jesus. God Himself appeared in the flame of fire. It is important to note here that the bush did not fuel the fire but the presence and glory of God was the single source.

It stopped Moses in his tracks. Whenever you experience the glory, you cannot settle for going back to your everyday existence. The glory of God will change you. Once you have tasted of it, you become addicted and cannot settle for less.

The movement that I see coming is set apart by the heaviness of His glory and backed by the weight of the *Triple Threat Anointing*. In the Book of Acts, we never see the early apostles watering down the power of God in order to make it palatable to those they were called to reach. Rather, they were demonstrating the power of God everywhere they went. The gifts of the Spirit were flowing freely and signs and wonders confirmed the message they were preaching. God longs to move in such a way again.

> *The entire universe is standing on tiptoe, yearning to see the unveiling of God's glorious sons and daughters!* (Romans 8:19 TPT)

All of Heaven is anticipating, yearning for God's children to become His glorious sons and daughters. It could read, "the manifestation of the sons of God."

Interestingly, the Greek word used for "unveiling" (*apokalypsis*) is the same word for the full title of the last book of the Bible, "The Revelation [Unveiling] of Jesus Christ." The created universe is but the backdrop for the dramatic appearing of God's sons and daughters unveiled with the glory of Jesus Christ upon them. The verb tense in the Greek text is clear that this "unveiling" is imminent, soon to happen, and destined to take place. Christ's glory will come to us, enter us, fill us, envelop us, and then be revealed through us as partakers of the glory. Although God will not share his glory with any other, we are no longer "another," for we are one with the Father, Son, and Holy Spirit through faith in Christ.[1]

For the kingdom of God is not in word but in power (1 Corinthians 4:20 NKJV).

God aches for His sons and daughters to demonstrate His power. We have been commissioned to do the works of Jesus and even greater works. We cannot fall into the trap of pleasing society and the religious sect, hiding His power in order to blend in with the world. God is raising up ones who will refuse to regulate the moving of the Holy Spirit by confining His work to a back room or, worse, shutting the door to Him altogether. There is no replacement for His presence. Good production and man's way of doing church is not the answer. Submission to God and obedience to His plan is the only way that you and I can walk in the *Triple Threat Anointing* and be a part of the movement that He showed to me.

Moses was marked by the encounter he had with God in the burning bush. He experienced God in a new way. He was so greatly impacted that he was obedient to go back to Egypt and face Pharaoh to demand the Hebrews' freedom. When God reveals His glory and you have a personal encounter with Him, obedience is the byproduct of such an encounter.

> *And Moses took his wife and his sons, and set them upon an ass, and he returned to the land of Egypt: and Moses took the rod of God in his hand* (Exodus 4:20).

Notice that his rod became the "rod of God." It became a vehicle to demonstrate the power of God and was used to work many miracles. God will take what you have in the natural and it will become supernatural.

> *The Lord said to Aaron, "Go into the wilderness to meet Moses." So he went and met him at the mountain of God (Sinai) and kissed him. Moses told Aaron all the words of the Lord with which*

He had sent him, and all the signs that He had commanded him to do (Exodus 4:27-28 AMP).

God commanded Moses to do signs in Egypt. This was a command, not an option. He didn't tell Moses, "You can perform signs and wonders if you feel like it." Neither did He say, "As long as it does not offend the Israelites whom you are trying to win over or embarrass you in front of Pharaoh." No, he was commanded to move out in power as it was instrumental in bringing revival to the Israelites and proving God's power to the Egyptians.

> *And Moses and Aaron went and gathered together all the elders of the children of Israel: and Aaron spake all the words which the Lord had spoken unto Moses, and did the signs in the sight of the people. And the people believed: and when they heard that the Lord had visited the children of Israel, and that he had looked upon their affliction, then they bowed their heads and worshipped* (Exodus 4:29-31).

"And the people believed." The people believed because of the words that God had given Moses but also the signs or the power of God in demonstration. People are hungry for the supernatural. They flock to movies or television shows about the supernatural. Why do we see this? Because the church has vacated our influence and minimized the gifts of the Spirit. In the modern church, we would rather

entertain you and make you feel good rather than do what God has commanded us to do in order to see miracles, signs, and wonders.

Let me share with you two firsthand examples of the *Triple Threat Anointing* that I have experienced in my services. One night at church, the Holy Spirit began to move. Many had filled the altar to receive ministry for a variety of conditions; however, two stood out most to me. The first one was a woman who was possessed with a demonic spirit. As my team and I began to pray for her, she began to vomit up this spirit. This is where a lot in the modern church would have checked out. However, we prayed more fervently until there was a manifestation of her freedom. We witnessed before our very eyes a great change in her physical appearance. The torment that had been etched upon her face was replaced with a visible, glowing peace that transformed her countenance. She was set free through the power of the name of Jesus!

The second one who stood out to me that night was a precious lady whose spine was deformed, preventing her from standing straight. As the glory of God filled the room and she raised up both hands in the air and began to worship, she suddenly felt a click in her back. At first, she thought she had injured herself further, but soon discovered that she was able to stand upright and was no longer in pain. The *Triple Threat Anointing* of salvation, deliverance, and healing was evident that night in the service, testified to by many others who had manifestations.

NOTE

1. Brian Simmons, *The Passion Translation* (Racine, Wisconsin: BroadStreet Publishing Group, LLC, 2017), footnote, Romans 8:19.

CHAPTER 3

---·○·---

THE FLOW

‖ OF THE TRIPLE THREAT ANOINTING ‖

Jesus is the greatest example of walking in the *Triple Threat Anointing*. In His ministry, He actively demonstrated all three manifestations. Salvation, healing, and deliverance were all present wherever Jesus went.

One of my favorite examples of Jesus flowing in the *Triple Threat Anointing* is the story of a woman whose entire world was turned upside down by her encounter with Jesus.

> *And a certain woman, which had an issue of blood twelve years, and had suffered many things of many physicians, and had spent all that she had, and was nothing bettered, but rather grew worse* (Mark 5:25-26).

This woman was dying. She had this issue of blood for twelve years. She had been to doctor after doctor and had spent all the money that she had. Nonetheless, she found herself worse off than she was before she even went to the doctors.

It is important to put this woman's story in the correct cultural context. She was considered "unclean" because of her condition. She was isolated from society in accordance with the religious law. So she was not only sick and broke from failed treatments, but she was also all alone. I can almost hear the sound of heartbreak that would ring out as she cried herself to sleep. I can picture the tears streaming down her face caused by the overwhelming loneliness that she suffered for twelve long years. She was living a hopeless existence day after day, year after year.

Then came the day she heard of Jesus. How she heard we do not know, but she did! She heard that Jesus performed miracles, mighty miracles. Faith rose up in this woman as she heard about the Miracle Worker. *"So then faith comes by hearing, and hearing by the word of God"* (Rom. 10:17 NKJV).

Whenever you find yourself leaking or being depleted, it is crucial that you fill yourself up with the Word of God. If you are facing opposition, the Bible has your answer for complete victory. As you hear the Word of God, it causes faith to be activated. We know that *faith* is how we please God according to the Book of Hebrews (see Heb. 11:6).

> *When she had heard of Jesus, came in the press behind, and touched his garment. For she said, If I may touch but his clothes, I shall be whole. And straightway the fountain of her blood was dried up; and she felt in her body that she was healed of that plague* (Mark 5:27-29 KJV).

Notice the sequence in this story:

- She *"heard"* (faith came into her).

- She came in *"behind"* (behind the people). I can imagine this was because of the shame of being ostracized and lawfully disqualified from being in such a crowded surrounding. But her faith caused her to keep moving forward! Faith will cause you to move into an arena that society or even the church may have excluded you from entering. I believe some individuals who have been "behind" in their destiny will suddenly be catapulted to the *forefront* because of their faith.

- She *"said."* Are you aware that it matters what you are saying? Are you rehearsing your circumstances and coming into agreement with the enemy's plan, or are you declaring God's Word over your situation? Stop agreeing with satan; instead, start agreeing with God by speaking and decreeing His Word by faith!

And Jesus, immediately knowing in Himself that power had gone out of Him, turned around in the crowd and said, "Who touched My clothes?" But His disciples said to Him, "You see the multitude thronging You, and You say, 'Who touched Me?'" And He looked around to see her who had done this thing. But the woman, fearing and trembling, knowing what had happened to her, came and fell down before Him and told Him the whole truth. And He said to her, "Daughter, your faith has made you well. Go in peace, and be healed of your affliction" (Mark 5:30-34 NKJV).

When the woman touched Him, Jesus recognized immediately that someone's faith had put a demand on His healing power. He asked the question, *"Who touched My clothes?"* The disciples were baffled that He asked this question. There were so many people in the multitude, all pressing and shoving just to get near Him. What set apart this woman was her faith and determination. It wasn't just that her fingers touched the hem of His garment. No, her faith had activated God's power and caused it to flow through Jesus to her.

I love the last verse of this woman's story. Jesus called her *"Daughter."* In doing so, He was in essence proclaiming, *She belongs to Me.* Remember, this woman felt unworthy. In fact, she trembled as she fell before Him, confessing what she had done. We are able to gain a clear perspective of the transformation that occurred in her life by simply looking at the progressive change in titles by which she was called. She went from being referred to as "a certain woman" to an unknown "who," as in "who touched my clothes?" and then finally to the highest elevation of being called "daughter" who was known by Him.

One of the first sermons that I ever preached was on this text. I have always wondered what her name was or what she was called. I even found it sad that she is always described by her condition and not her faith. We always think of her name as being the "Woman with the Issue of Blood." I asked the Lord one day, "Why did You allow us to only know her by the condition from which she was healed? After You made her whole, it somehow seems unfair to keep bringing up her issue. She was no longer the old her. She was a new creation. I wouldn't want the world calling me by the issues from which You freed me." He said to me, *"Look again. I did not say, 'Woman with the issue of blood, your faith has made you whole.' No, I called her My Daughter."* That was powerful to me. And I would say that you, too, are not defined by your condition or who you used to be. You are His child, a joint heir with Christ.

This story concluded with Jesus saying to her, His daughter, "your faith hath made you whole." The word translated *whole,* according to Strong's Concordance, is the Greek word *sozo,* which means "to save, deliver, protect, heal preserve, do well, make whole." When Jesus said, "Daughter, your faith has made you whole," He was announcing to her that she had been saved, healed, and delivered. This was the *Triple Threat Anointing* in action!

CHAPTER 4

—●•○•●—

EXPECTATION

‖ THE EXPECTANT HEART ‖

One day when I was thirteen years old, my father came home from work and was not feeling well. He went to bed and did not get up for the rest of that day. The next morning, I went into his room to check on him. It was very unusual for him to be sick and even more unusual for him to not get up to go to work. When I walked into his room, I immediately knew something was terribly wrong. All of the color had drained from his face. He was sweating profusely and screamed out in agony when I barely touched him. I hurriedly took his temperature and found that it was extremely high. I begged him to go to the small emergency room that was near our house. He refused to go, believing that he would be fine with some rest. Later that day, when I returned home from school,

I discovered that his condition had worsened. He finally consented to go to the emergency room.

When we arrived at the hospital, the medical professionals quickly realized that this was not the flu. They explained to us that they were going to transfer him by ambulance to Memorial Hospital, one of Chattanooga's larger hospitals, so he could receive more aggressive treatment. There he was placed in the Intensive Care Unit. My grandmother drove me down to the hospital and waited for what seemed like an eternity in my thirteen-year-old mind. My sister and brother-in-law arrived shortly thereafter. The doctors would not let us in to see him. I could not understand what was transpiring. Our thoughts and emotions were all over the place.

Finally, one of the doctors came out to share his diagnosis. He explained that they did not know what was making him sick. His tests had all come back negative and they were mystified by his condition. They did not know what to expect or how to treat this mystery illness. This news left us feeling discouraged and despondent. How could they not know what was going on? Why are we going through this? Where are You, God? These questions plagued our mind.

After that, my sister and I were allowed to go into the tiny room to visit with him for thirty minutes, every three hours. We walked into his room and could barely recognize him. His appearance had severely changed.

His skin looked a strange greenish color and he had tiny red dots all over his body. His hands and feet had swollen so severely that the skin on his fingers and toes split open and blood shot forth from his fingertips and toes. This couldn't be my father. He was exceptionally healthy. He was extremely disciplined in his diet and exercise. Although we couldn't recognize him through his physical appearance, we knew his voice as he spoke, comforting us. He tried his best to put on a brave face for us, even joking about his fingers and toes, but the seriousness of the situation was blatantly obvious.

I left the hospital that afternoon to go home and get some clothes in order to spend the night at the hospital. I walked into my bedroom, and as I packed some clothes into a bag, a picture that was framed in my bedroom caught my eye. It was a picture of me standing with my dad that had been taken just a year before. I will never forget this moment as long as I live. I grabbed the photograph and held it up toward Heaven. I said, "God, I know You are the God of miracles. I need a miracle. My father cannot die. He will live and not die, and declare the works of the Lord." I cannot accurately describe what happened in that moment other than to say that the presence of God filled that room. Suddenly, I felt a strong release, and an unexplainable peace came over me. I knew that God had heard and answered me.

We went back to the hospital to spend the night. The doctor pulled us aside before we were allowed to enter the ICU for the last visitation of the night. He said, "Take your time during this visit. His condition has worsened and he will most likely not make it through the night." The waiting area at the time was in a round corridor that was surrounded with windows. I remember staring vacantly at the lights in the parking lot as he told us the worst news that we could imagine. My older sister fell to the ground sobbing. My grandmothers were both crying. I bent down, helping my sister to her feet while trying to comfort her at the same time. Right then, a boldness rose up in me and before I knew it the words flew out of my mouth, "I do not receive that report. He will live and not die and declare the works of the Lord. God told me that he will not die from this." The doctor did not know how to respond to my outburst, and it was fine with me because I was done talking to him.

After my great faith proclamation, nothing changed. He did not rise up from the hospital bed. Revival did not break out in the hospital. Instead, things became worse, as they often do whenever you are contending for a promise. We were told that they believed that he had somehow been infected with spinal meningitis. There had recently been several deaths from the virus in our area. We knew this was not good. There were many times that it was touch and go. We did not know what to presume day after day, and yet we believed. We fully expected that somehow God would bring forth a miracle. My sister and I did not leave the hospital except to shower and change clothes. Night after night, we slept in the ICU waiting room in cold leather recliners. Every time we would hear the nurses give the call "code blue" over the intercom system, our hearts would race. Is that our dad?

Almost every night, like clockwork, when it was time for the last visit, the doctor gave us the same warning, "He most likely will not make it through the night." Every time that he would say it, I would rebuke it. I had a promise from God, and I would not let anyone make me doubt it. I knew that God had heard my cry that day when I held that picture in the air and prayed at the top of my lungs. There were many people praying and standing in agreement with us. We knew that it was done and our dad would be returning home.

There were a lot of ups and downs during this time. Moments of great faith and some of being wearied from standing. Evangelist Perry Stone, a close family friend, was in the middle of preaching a revival but flew into Chattanooga to come to the hospital to pray for him. When he came out of the room, he prophetically confirmed everything God had spoken to me. In fact, he was so confident of his full recovery that he went back to preach his revival services. It was another confirmation to me that it was done.

After several weeks in the ICU, he was moved to a regular room in the hospital and then eventually allowed to come home. It took a year until he would fully recover. Nonetheless, he is alive today, completely whole, and is declaring the works of the Lord, just as God promised.

If you are facing circumstances that are contrary to what God has spoken to you, stand strong in faith, declaring the Word of God. Don't ever lose your expectation that God is fulfilling every promise that He has made to you. If He spoke it, He will bring to pass. Pastor Rod Parsley has said "Expectation is the breeding ground for miracles." Get your hopes up and *expect* God to do the impossible. Your expectation births your miracle.

Religion hates the expectant heart. Why? Real expectation in the heart of an individual provokes a response. Those who have camped in dead religion want everyone to settle there along with them. It affronts those who live in the dead religion camp to see someone else break out of the boundaries that have confined them.

It was the religious rulers who were cunningly motivated to kill Jesus to try to stop this movement. They were terrified of losing their positions and control of the people. It was the same religious sect who, later, forcefully tried to halt His disciples from preaching in His name. They were blinded by fear, steeped in religious traditions, and captivated by their own positions of authority. They willingly settled for a dead, powerless religious institution, loving their status in society more than embracing what God was doing in the "now moment."

The sad thing is that we still see this in today's church world. We have mega churches that have rejected the Holy Spirit or tried to box Him in to fit their formats and time schedules. I am not railing against large ministries. In fact, I believe in the coming *Triple Threat Movement* we will see even larger churches, networks, and gatherings than ever before. Those who have plugged in to the power source of the Holy Spirit will experience supernatural growth and multiplication much like we read about in the Book of Acts.

After the upper room outpouring of the Holy Spirit, we see multiple examples of the *Triple Threat Anointing* being demonstrated as a principle in the early Church.

Now Peter and John went up together into the temple at the hour of prayer, being the ninth hour. And a certain man lame from his mother's womb was carried, whom they laid daily at the gate of the temple which is called Beautiful, to ask alms of them that entered into the temple; who seeing Peter and John about to go into the temple asked an alms. And Peter, fastening his eyes upon him with John, said, Look on us. And he gave heed unto them, expecting to receive something of them. Then Peter said, Silver and gold have I none; but such as I have give I thee: In the name of Jesus Christ of Nazareth rise up and walk. And he took him by the right hand, and lifted him up: and immediately his feet and ankle bones received strength. And he leaping up stood, and walked, and entered with them into the temple, walking, and leaping, and praising God. And all the people saw him walking and praising God: and they knew that it was he which sat for alms at the Beautiful gate of the temple: and they were filled with wonder and amazement at that which had happened unto him (Acts 3:1-10).

After the Lord spoke to me about the *Triple Threat Anointing,* I was able to see a deeper revelation of the above Scripture passage, which by the way happens to be one of my favorite stories in the Bible. Note that the account of this miracle began with the word *now.* The meaning of the word *now,* as used in the instance when the paralyzed man walked, could be defined as "in view of the fact," meaning that something happened before this demonstration of power. What fact had transpired before this miracle? Peter and John had received the *dunamis* power of the Holy Spirit, causing their ministry to take on a new dimension. "Now" they looked through the lens of the Holy Spirit. It heavily communicated the weight of the glory that they were now carrying. Whenever you begin to see through the Spirit's eyes, everything changes.

The lame man had been in this condition *"from his mother's womb."* This passage described that he was laid daily at the gate of the Temple to beg from the ones who entered in. When I imagine this man laying "outside the temple," it saddens my heart, causing me to think about those whom the Church rejects, simply because they do not fit into their cliques or clubs. Why were the religious group satisfied with leaving him outside of the temple? Why do some churches today still reject people based on their appearance, past, or background? We have to recognize that in this coming new move, God will be sending the millionaire and the homeless. He will be raising up the ones in the three-piece suits as well as the ones wearing ill-fitted, worn clothing. It is not up to us to decide who God chooses to bless or who He decides to use.

We see that Peter and John were walking into the temple when this lame beggar began asking for money. The text says, *"And Peter, fastening his eyes upon him with John, said, Look on us."* In other words, "Get a new vision. Today, God is going to do something new in your life." It goes on to say that this lame man was *"expecting to receive something."* Does this excite your faith? It does mine. He had an expectant heart. However, he only expected what he had known up until this point. He expected them to give him some alms, as all the other religious people had done, day after day. God wanted to stretch his expectation, even as He wants to stretch yours, too! Some of you may have been expecting "something"—that something being in the same realm that you have always received—but by divine appointment God is challenging you through this book to "look" through the lens of the Holy Spirit beyond the expected physical realm into the supernatural realm! Exceed your expectation! God is saying to you, *"Today is your day!"*

Peter said, *"Silver and gold have I none."* In other words, "I don't have what you are expecting; instead, I have something much better. *In the name of Jesus Christ of Nazareth rise up and walk."* This is radical faith in motion. Peter is telling this man to do what he had never been able to do. God will stretch you to do something you have never done before to show forth His power.

> *And he took him by the right hand, and lifted him up: and immediately his feet and ankle bones received strength. And he leaping up stood, and walked, and entered with them into the temple, walking, and leaping, and praising God* (Acts 3:7-8).

It is very interesting that they took him by the right hand. The right hand signifies authority. Jesus is seated at the right hand of the Father.

> *But he, being full of the Holy Ghost, looked up stedfastly into heaven, and saw the glory of God, and Jesus standing on the right hand of God, and said, Behold, I see the heavens opened, and the Son of man standing on the right hand of God* (Acts 7:55-56).

Now the main point of what we are saying is this: We do have such a high priest, who sat down at the right hand of the throne of the Majesty in heaven (Hebrews 8:1 NIV).

Looking to Jesus, the founder and perfecter of our faith, who for the joy that was set before him endured the cross, despising the shame, and is seated at the right hand of the throne of God (Hebrews 12:2 ESV).

This lame man did not walk in authority. He was a beggar, lame and could not get up, but when Peter took him by the right hand, Peter demonstrated the weight of authority that comes through the name of Jesus and by the power of the Holy Spirit. Acts 3:7-8 says, *"immediately his feet and ankle bones received strength"* and *"he leaping up stood, and walked."* Pay attention to the words *now* and *immediately* in this story because they refer to timing. This man had suffered with this condition for years, and then bam, a "suddenly" happens. Have you, too, dealt with something your whole life that's life-altering like the lame man? Right now, God can perform an *immediately,* a *suddenly,* and an *unexpected* in your life, too. Did you know that God has already planned your day of deliverance?

I also am in awe of the completeness of this miracle. They did not pull him up by his right hand for him to wobble around and fall back down. No, the man who had never used his legs, ankles, or feet immediately began "*jumping, leaping and praising God.*" Think about it. There was no long rehab for this man; instead, God immediately and completely made him well. God still does creative miracles. He desires for you to be whole, complete, and wanting nothing.

Peter then began to preach the Gospel to all who were gathered there witnessing the man totally healed. The religious hierarchy was riled that the disciples preached the resurrection of Jesus. They were desperate to shut down this Jesus movement. They arrested both Peter and John, but not before 5,000 men, not including women and children, were saved.

> But many of those who heard the message [of salvation] believed [in Jesus and accepted Him as the Christ]. And the number of the men came to be about 5,000 (Acts 4:4 AMP).

It is hard for us today to fully realize the enormous magnitude of this miracle—5,000 men "heard" the message of salvation. We could stop right there and that in itself is extraordinary. How do 5,000 men hear an orator with no microphone to amplify his voice? One could reason that there must have been great acoustics where they were gathered, and that was probably true, but we must not discount that Peter's voice was amplified by the Holy Spirit in order to fulfill God's purpose.

I have come to the conclusion that Jesus and Peter must have been loud preachers. Personally, I love that, and one reason I do is because when I first started preaching, I had two pastors sit me down in their office and proceeded to give me a list with 50 critiques of my ministry. It was not given out of love to help me to be more effective, but rather to break my confidence and zeal for what God had called me to do. There is a big difference in a loving spiritual mother or father giving you constructive feedback and one who has a critical, religious spirit criticizing you. On this list were things such as "you sweat too much." How do you control sweat? The silliness of these criticisms shows the motives behind what they were saying.

They went on to say, "You get too excited when you preach; you need to be calmer" and "you are too loud." As they went over this list point by point, I could feel my confidence being chipped away with every word that was coming from their mouth. Thoughts plagued my mind: *Maybe they are right. Why can't you just stand behind the pulpit and preach a nice message? Why do you have to be so enthusiastic when the Holy Spirit comes on you? Why do you have such a big voice?* As I left the pastor's office, I knew what David was talking about when he spoke of his soul being downcast. I was convinced I was useless to the kingdom of God. As I reached for the doorknob of the main entrance of the church, I heard the Holy Spirit speak to me. He said, *"Andrew, quit trying to force-feed people who are not hungry for what you carry. Shake the dust off your feet. There are people dying for what I have put inside of you."* In the church parking lot, I actually took my shoes off and shook them as a prophetic act.

Dust will always try to cling to your feet whenever God is calling you to step into a new season. Dust is made up of tiny particles from where you have been (your last season). The dust of yesterday will try to pollute you as you walk into the new of where God is taking you. Have you ever walked in a place where there was dirt? The first thing you want to do is shake it off of you. My mother enforces a rule in her home. Whenever we go to her house, we are expected to remove our shoes at the door or put on the paper booties over our shoes. She knows that wherever our shoes have been, they have collected particles, and those particles would track in with us and pollute her clean house. We do not have this rule at our house, but I see the effectiveness of her requirement. Much like this example, God will not allow you to carry the past into your future. Shake it off, for it will surely pollute the next place into which God leads you.

My loud, demonstrative style of preaching makes me different. It may not be everyone's flavor, but I am okay with that—it is for the ones whom I am called to reach. I am not loud just to be loud. I cannot help but become enthusiastic when I start talking about God. As the church moves in the *Triple Threat Anointing*, it will require everyone's gifts and talents. We should not only embrace diversity but celebrate it.

After Peter and John were used to heal the lame beggar and preached the sermon that won 5,000 men to the Lord, they were arrested and placed in hold until the next day.

> *While Peter and John were addressing the people, the priests, the chief of the Temple police, and some Sadducees came up, indignant that these upstart apostles were instructing the people and proclaiming that the resurrection from the dead had taken place in Jesus. They arrested them and threw them in jail until morning, for by now it was late in the evening. But many of those who listened had already believed the Message—in round numbers about five thousand!* (Acts 4:1-4 MSG)

The spirit of religion becomes indignant when God disrupts their "business as usual" routine. The purpose of the spirit of religion is to entrap believers into a cold state of Christianity or, even worse, to validate them into becoming lukewarm.

> *I know your works, that you are neither cold nor hot. I could wish you were cold or hot. So then because you are lukewarm, and neither cold nor hot, I will vomit you out of My mouth* (Revelation 3:15-16 NKJV).

The religious spirit thrives on passionless worship and churches void of the presence of God. It fuels lethargic believers into believing that stale Christianity is all there is in God. It hurls lies, screaming to the spiritual zombies who are in its clutches: *There is nothing more from God for you. It's normal to be dry spiritually. You are fine. Everyone compromises.* Don't listen to the devil's lies! I declare to you today, "There is more in God. He wants to reveal Himself to you in a new way. He wants to refill you with the Holy Spirit today. Seek Him and you will find Him."

After Peter and John were arrested for preaching the Gospel, their captors were forced to let them go. Most Christians would go undercover at this point. They would lay low, in fear of rocking the boat or instigating more persecution. Not these world changers; they decided to have a prayer meeting. I often say, "Prayer births every move of God, and it also sustains every move of God." You will never see a genuine move of the Holy Spirit that was not preceded by prayer. Prayer declares our absolute dependence on God. The power that Jesus walked in can be traced to His prayer life and constant communication with His Father.

> *And being let go, they went to their own companions and reported all that the chief priests and elders had said to them. So when they heard that, they raised their voice to God with one accord and said: "Lord, You are God, who made heaven and*

earth and the sea, and all that is in them, who by the mouth of Your servant David have said: 'Why did the nations rage, and the people plot vain things? The kings of the earth took their stand, and the rulers were gathered together against the Lord and against His Christ.' For truly against Your holy Servant Jesus, whom You anointed, both Herod and Pontius Pilate, with the Gentiles and the people of Israel, were gathered together to do whatever Your hand and Your purpose determined before to be done. Now, Lord, look on their threats, and grant to Your servants that with all boldness they may speak Your word, by stretching out Your hand to heal, and that signs and wonders may be done through the name of Your holy Servant Jesus." And when they had prayed, the place where they were assembled together was shaken; and they were all filled with the Holy Spirit, and they spoke the word of God with boldness (Acts 4:23-31 NKJV).

These disciples were not playing. They were not lying around in self-pity about what they had been through. No, they called a prayer meeting and issued a call to arms for the saints. Notice that they described the "threats" of the religious rulers, but instead of watering down their message they asked God for more boldness, more signs and wonders. The modern church can, and should, do the same.

We need more of the power of God and less fear of offending people. People are hungry for the supernatural. This is the reason why we see great numbers of people going to movies and reading books that have supernatural themes. The problem is that in seeking for something deeper they are tapping into the wrong supernatural realm.

The Church needs to ask God for a greater flow of His Spirit and to multiply supernatural signs and wonders rather than settling for a powerless church. We do not have to restrict the Holy Spirit to see growth. This story of the lame man at the Gate Beautiful reveals to us God's plan for church growth—it is through the power and demonstration of the Holy Spirit.

But ye shall receive power, after that the Holy Ghost is come upon you: and ye shall be witnesses unto me both in Jerusalem, and in all Judaea, and in Samaria, and unto the uttermost part of the earth (Acts 1:8).

The Greek word *dunamis* has been translated into the English Bible as *power*. According to the Dake's Anointed Reference Bible, it is defined as "inherent power capable of reproducing itself like a dynamo." It is where the word *dynamite* comes from. In other words, Jesus was saying, "After the Holy Ghost comes upon you, then you will have dynamite power." I don't know about you but I have never seen a calm outburst of dynamite. No, it is explosive. It cannot be tamed. Like the early Church, we, today, need more *dunamis* power in our lives.

> *And when they had prayed, the place was shaken where they were assembled together; and they were all filled with the Holy Ghost, and they spake the word of God with boldness* (Acts 4:31).

God shook the place, when they prayed, and they were all filled with the Holy Ghost. These apostles and Christian believers had already been filled with the Holy Ghost but needed a refilling. How long has it been since you sought another refilling of the Holy Ghost in your life? A lot of times we are so focused on targeting our desires for natural things in prayer that we omit asking for the supernatural things of God. I believe this is the time for another room-shaking, Holy Ghost-refilling outpour from God. We have not because we ask not. Start praying for God to move in you and through you.

Let's get back to the movement of the *Triple Threat Anointing* in this story of the outpouring of the Holy Spirit and the refilling of the early disciples. It is found in the following passage of Scripture:

> *And by the hands of the apostles were many signs and wonders wrought among the people; (and they were all with one accord in Solomon's porch. And of the rest durst no man join himself to them: but the people magnified them. And believers*

were the more added to the Lord, multitudes both of men and women.) Insomuch that they brought forth the sick into the streets, and laid them on beds and couches, that at the least the shadow of Peter passing by might overshadow some of them (Acts 5:12-15).

Believers were added to the Lord, multitudes, both men and women—by this we can see mass *salvation*.

There came also a multitude out of the cities round about unto Jerusalem, bringing sick folks, and them which were vexed with unclean spirits: and they were healed every one (Acts 5:16).

By this verse we can see mass *healings* of the sick, as well as mass *deliverances* of those who were vexed of unclean spirits.

Acts 5:12-16 sums up the *Triple Threat Anointing* that is available for every believer to carry.

1. Salvation
2. Healings
3. Deliverances

As you read this book, I am believing that the Holy Spirit is recharging your expectation levels. Right now, all you have to do is just simply ask Him to refill you and empower you to walk in a greater level of boldness.

This is your time to walk in the authority of the *Triple Threat Anointing!*

CHAPTER 5

—◉—

SEEING WITH SUPERNATURAL EYES

‖ The Triple Threat Anointing ‖

One Sunday morning as I was preaching, an elderly lady who suffered with an eye condition that left her legally blind all of a sudden began shouting, "I can see. I can see." Her interruption did not come during the altar service or even in a healing line, but instead it came right in the middle of my message! I was stunned, but recognized it as a Holy Spirit divine interruption.

The subject I was ministering on was faith. The Bible says, *"So then faith comes by hearing, and hearing by the word of God"* (Rom. 10:17). She heard the Word of God and it activated her faith. She neither had hands laid on her nor a prayer spoken over her. She simply rose up in faith and received her healing through the preaching of His Word.

This precious lady had been believing God for a miracle for years. She had been in numerous prayer lines, but the condition only grew worse with each passing year. However, something unusual happened that day. She heard, she received, and she claimed the promise of God! It was clear to me that the Holy Spirit wanted to do more than just preach the Word that morning; He wanted to demonstrate the Word. He moved to orchestrate the service, and I followed His lead. I begin to lay hands on the sick and started praying for them. There was an explosion of healing that took place in that service.

One of the other instances of the *Triple Threat Anointing* that we see in the ministry of Jesus is recorded in the Gospel of Matthew.

And when Jesus departed thence, two blind men followed him, crying, and saying, Thou son of David, have mercy on us. And when he was come into the house, the blind men came to him: and Jesus saith unto them, Believe ye that I am able to do this? They said unto him, Yea, Lord. Then touched he their eyes, saying, According to your faith be it unto you. And their eyes were opened; and Jesus straitly charged them, saying, See that no man know it. But they, when they were departed, spread abroad his fame in all that country. As they went out, behold, they brought to him a dumb man possessed with a devil. And when the devil was cast out, the dumb spake: and the multitudes marvelled, saying, It was never so seen in Israel. But the Pharisees said, He casteth out devils through the prince of the devils (Matthew 9:27-34).

The two blind men came to Jesus, crying, *"Son of David."* This was a bold declaration. They were not just saying, "Jesus," "Prophet," or "Miracle Worker," but with that statement they were declaring His deity—that He, indeed, was the promised Messiah (Salvation). It is a profound truth that although these men could not see with their *natural eyes,* they could see with their *spiritual eyes,* and what they clearly saw was that Jesus Christ was the Son of God! Don't ever discount someone you would never choose. God can reveal Himself to whomever He chooses.

Jesus first asked them a question: *"Believe ye that I am able to do this?"* They answered, *"Yea, Lord."* Do you remember Chapter Four on *expectation?* These men fall into that category of expectation. They believed that Jesus was the promised Messiah and that He could do what they were requesting. I love how verse 29 reads in *The Passion Translation* Bible, *"Then Jesus put his hands over their eyes and said, 'You will have what your faith expects!'"* You too, will have what your faith expects!

And instantly their eyes opened—they could see! Then Jesus warned them sternly, "Make sure that you tell no one what just happened!" But unable to contain themselves, they went out and spread the news everywhere! (Matthew 9:30-31 TPT)

After they received their sight and Jesus demonstrated that He, indeed, was the Messiah, He then instructed them not to tell anyone. He did this because He had not yet completed His assignment on earth. It was simply not yet time for Him to be offered as the sacrificial Lamb, paying the price for our sins. However, these men, bubbling over with excitement, could not help themselves; they had to tell what had just happened to them!

While they were leaving, some people brought before Jesus a man with a demon spirit who couldn't speak. Jesus cast the demon out of him, and immediately the man began to speak plainly. The crowds marveled in astonishment, saying, "We've never seen miracles like this in Israel!" But the Pharisees kept saying, "The chief of demons is helping him drive out demons" (Matthew 9:32-34 TPT).

We have seen the salvation and healing anointing with the blind men. Now we get a glimpse of the deliverance anointing with this mute man. All sickness is of the enemy. God does not put sickness on us to teach us a lesson or to humble us. I have often heard it said, "If it wasn't God-sent, it will still be God-used," meaning that God will take what satan has meant for our evil and turn it around for our good. The story of Job clearly reveals to us that sickness and loss is from the devil, and yet God allowed it in the case of Job. But the good news is that although God allowed it, in the end God rewarded Job, and he came out of his season of testing with double.

Some cases of sickness, as in the mute man, are caused by possession of a demonic spirit. Other sickness is caused by the law of nature or by poor decisions with our health. When I was a little boy, my parents were pastors of a local church in Chattanooga, Tennessee. I remember a particular prayer service where the Holy Spirit was moving in a powerful way. A man who did not attend our church walked over to a dear lady who was in a wheelchair and he started rebuking the devil out of her. He was screaming that she was possessed with the devil and that was why she was in the wheelchair. The only problem was that she was not demon possessed. She was a woman of God. Her accident was caused when she dove into the shallow end of a pool and hit her head, thus breaking her neck in the process, which left her paralyzed. My mother quickly corrected the man, but he would not relent. My father ended up escorting him out of the service. It made a big impression on me as a boy. We must have discernment between a spirit of infirmity and natural circumstances. Not everyone has a devil. Whether it is a devil or natural occurrence that has caused sickness, know for certain it is always God's will to heal.

We must be willing to operate in the same anointing as Jesus did if we want to see the move of God. Jesus was not afraid of the lost, the sick, or those who were possessed by demon spirits. You may be saying, "Of course not. He was God." He was also all man. Jesus laid aside all of His godly attributes of omniscience (all-knowingness), omnipresence (present everywhere at the same time), and omnipotence (all powerful) and operated on the earth as a man empowered by the Holy Spirit. He did not do the miracles He did because He was God, but He did them as a man anointed by the Spirit of God, and we can too!

> Though he was God, he did not think of equality with God as something to cling to. Instead, he gave up his divine privileges; he took the humble position of a slave and was born as a human being. When he appeared in human form (Philippians 2:6-7 NLT).

Take note that Jesus did not walk in the *Triple Threat Anointing* or begin His public ministry until John baptized Him. It was during this holy act of obedience that the *heavenly realm* opened up to and over Him and the Holy Spirit came upon Him.

And as Jesus rose up out of the water, the heavenly realm opened up over him and he saw the Holy Spirit descend out of the heavens and rest upon him in the form of a dove (Matthew 3:16 TPT).

He was anointed as a man by the power of the Holy Spirit. He was all man because He chose to lay down His Godly attributes to become *"the Son of Man."* The same Holy Spirit who lives in us was the same Holy Spirit who came and rested upon Him. God is declaring to you right now that His desire is to open up the heavenly realm over your life.

The Spirit of God, who raised Jesus from the dead, lives in you. And just as God raised Christ Jesus from the dead, he will give life to your mortal bodies by this same Spirit living within you (Romans 8:11 NLT).

The Bible instructs us to "desire" to walk in the gifts of the Spirit. Having the gifts of the Spirit manifest in your life always begins with "desire." The main takeaway from this book that I pray every reader receives is that there is more to God. You will never come to a place where you have experienced all there is of Him. He will never become old to you as long as you are walking in alignment with Him. Living as a child of God and being led by the Spirit is one of the most exciting things anyone could ever do.

*Pursue [this] love [with eagerness, make it your goal], yet earnestly **desire** and cultivate the spiritual gifts [to be used by believers for the benefit of the church], but especially that you may prophesy [to foretell the future, to speak a new message from God to the people]* (1 Corinthians 14:1 AMP).

*Therefore I say unto you, What things soever ye **desire**, when ye pray, believe that ye receive them, and ye shall have them* (Mark 11:24).

In the above Scripture, the word translated as *desire* from the original Greek means to "ask, beg, call for, crave, desire, or require." What does this say to you? It says that you have to cultivate and mature these gifts by allowing the Holy Spirit to flow through you.

I believe that many of you reading this book are being stirred to go to another level in God. He wants to reveal Himself to you. He is longing to show forth His power in your life.

And when He had called His twelve disciples to Him, He gave them power over unclean spirits, to cast them out, and to heal all kinds of sickness and all kinds of disease (Matthew 10:1 NKJV).

And as you go, preach, saying, "The kingdom of heaven is at hand." Heal the sick, raise the dead, cleanse the lepers, cast out demons. Freely you have received, freely give (Matthew 10:7-8 AMP).

In the above verse, we read of the first time that Jesus gave the twelve disciples the power of the *Triple Threat Anointing*. Observe how He instructed the twelve to move in the *Triple Threat Anointing*—He told them to preach, "The kingdom of God is at hand," the message of repentance (salvation); *"heal the sick"* (healing); and *"cast out demons"* (deliverance).

Although I am prophetically writing a revelation of the future movement that is coming, this anointing was given to the disciples and is available now to you and I. We have no more defenses of why we are not moving in this *Triple Threat Anointing*.

CHAPTER 6

NO MORE EXCUSES

|| It Is Time for the Miraculous ||

After this there was a feast of the Jews; and Jesus went up to Jerusalem. Now there is at Jerusalem by the sheep market a pool, which is called in the Hebrew tongue Bethesda, having five porches. In these lay a great multitude of impotent folk, of blind, halt, withered, waiting for the moving of the water. For an angel went down at a certain season into the pool, and troubled the water: whosoever then first after the troubling of the water stepped in was made whole of whatsoever disease he had. And a certain man was there, which had an infirmity thirty and eight years. When Jesus saw him lie, and knew that he had been now a long time in that case, he saith unto him, Wilt thou be made whole? The impotent man answered him, Sir, I have no man, when the water is troubled, to put me into the pool: but while I am coming, another steppeth down before

*me. Jesus saith unto him, Rise, take up thy bed,
and walk. And immediately the man was made
whole, and took up his bed, and walked: and on
the same day was the sabbath* (John 5:1-9).

This story has always been fascinating to me. As a
pastor and an itinerate minister, I often am in contact
with people such as this man. I have even found this man's
traits in myself. We all can make excuses. We are good at
giving reasons why we aren't further along and why we
don't have time to spend in prayer or the Word. We are
gifted at explaining why we aren't seeing souls saved, the
sick healed, and the captives delivered.

I can relate to this man who sat by the pool of
Bethesda. He was a lot like us—full of excuses. I think
it is so interesting that Jesus saw him and asked him a
question: "Will you be made whole?" We may read that
and think, *Isn't that obvious? Why would Jesus ask him
that? The man is sick. Yes, of course he wants to be made
whole.* But Jesus never did anything by coincidence.
He was asking this man to make a decision. We are one
decision away from seeing the greatest move of God this
world has ever seen, but God is waiting for you and I to
make the decision and answer Him with a "yes." Your
"yes" to God can turn the world upside down. You may
be saying, "I have been saved for 20 years. What are you
talking about?" I am talking about a complete surrender

to God's plan and becoming vessels of honor that He can use to show the world His power.

This man had his "infirmity" for 38 years. The Greek word translated *infirmity* means "feebleness (of body or mind)." Yes, he was sick in his body, but he was also dealing with the strongholds in his mind. He had dealt with this problem for a long time. Remember, he was surrounded by "*a great multitude of impotent folk, of blind, halt, withered, waiting for the moving of the water*" (John 5:3). The people who surrounded him were just like him. There was no one there urging him on, telling him that he was meant for greater things and that God could heal him. No, they just all suffered together. They all had the mindset that it was their lot in life. He didn't feel out of place. Everyone was in the same boat. No one was saying in his ear, *God has called you for greater.* His friends, and even those who surrounded him who were spiritual, never pushed him to go higher with God. He needed people in his life who were "salt and light." Salt will make one thirsty and light will expose dark areas in one's life. He needed to be around people who would sharpen him so that he, in return, could sharpen them. It mattered who surrounded him! It also matters who surrounds you.

It was there at the pool that they lay or sat, day after day, just "waiting" for a supernatural occurrence to happen. We, too, often "wait" for something to happen when God is waiting on us to make something happen.

You are a carrier of change. You have been called to shift atmospheres and to release God's glory here on the earth. We are waiting for revival, but God says, *"You are the revival."*

The impotent man answered Jesus' question, *"The impotent man answered him, Sir, I have no man, when the water is troubled, to put me into the pool: but while I am coming, another steppeth down before me"* (John 5:7).

Even as I am writing this, it stings me a little bit because I can see myself in the impotent man's answer. He answered Jesus' very straightforward question with what seemed like really logical reasons why he was not made whole. He said, "I have no man to put me into the pool. When God is moving, there's just no one to help me." One time I was going through a difficult time in ministry. I was extremely frustrated. Nothing seemed to be happening for me. It felt like every door had been closed to me. I had promises from God, but everything seemed to be happening the very opposite of what God had spoken. During that time, I was tempted with envy. I would see others whom God was blessing and I became negative, thinking to myself, *It must be nice. If I had that well-known minister helping me, I would be further along, too, but no one helps me. I'm out here by myself, isolated and alone.* Now, I know that was not the case, but when you are feeling the weight of pressure, it's easy for your mind to go down this path.

The impotent man then went on to say, "While I am coming, another steps down before me." In other words, "It's someone else's fault." God is the Promoter, not man. If man does it, then man can also take it away. It is better to wait on God. One of my life Scriptures is, *"That which is born of the flesh is flesh; and that which is born of the Spirit is spirit"* (John 3:6).

I love how it is translated in the New Living Translation: *"Humans can reproduce only human life, but the Holy Spirit gives birth to spiritual life."* Let me personalize that—what *you* birth in the flesh has to be maintained in the flesh, but what *you* birth by the Spirit will be maintained by the Spirit!

If you are a pastor, or a leader of any group, it is easy to *explain* why this is happening or why that isn't happening. One day in prayer, I found myself rationalizing this or that, when the Holy Spirit spoke very clearly to me, *"It is not because of this or that, this person or that person; it is simply because you have not birthed what I have spoken."* Talk about getting your toes stepped on! I felt like I had no toes left. There is no more time for excuses! We are living in an accelerated time. This is the time to birth a move of God. And God will partner with us as long as we die to flesh and follow His lead.

> *For all who are led by the Spirit of God are children of God* (Romans 8:14 NLT).

Jesus ignored this man's excuses. God doesn't want a list of excuses of why we can't possibly carry out His will and bring forth this revival; rather, He is looking for our "yes." He doesn't need the super talented, the best educated, or the most beautiful. No, He wants those through whom He can shine His light. He is looking for those to whom He can show Himself strong. We serve a mighty God, and there is nothing too hard for Him.

For the eyes of the Lord run to and fro throughout the whole earth, to shew himself strong in the behalf of them whose heart is perfect toward him (2 Chronicles 16:9).

After His dialogue with the impotent man, Jesus then commanded the man, saying, "Rise, take up your bed and walk!" I love how He did not entertain this man's excuses. He would not give in to the sick man's misfortunate circumstances. In essence, Jesus said to him, "Move past all of that. Be who and what God has called you to be." God is also telling you the same thing, saying, *"Move past your bad breaks in life. I have called you to be an overcomer."* You, too, are more than a conqueror. Jesus told the impotent man to *rise.* He also is telling you who are in a *low position* to rise up. He's saying to you, "Get up from the brokenness. Get up from the disappointment and the confusion. Today is your day to rise."

"Take up your bed and walk," Jesus said. It always puzzled me why Jesus told him to pick up his bed. If he had been bound to it for 38 years, then you would think he would want to burn that bed. By these words, Jesus was telling the man, "Master that which mastered you! Take up that bed and let it bear testimony that you use to be bound, but you're now free by the power of God."

The story of the impotent man being healed didn't stop there! It continued on with the Pharisees being greatly angered that this man was healed on the Sabbath day. This is a picture of the spirit of religion hating a new move of God. They would rather have this man sick and bound to his bed than to move past the old way of doing things and have God move in a new fashion. I would like to say that this doesn't still happen in the Church, but unfortunately it does. We have to be free from our religious traditions and allow the Holy Spirit to move the way He wants to move.

One Sunday morning at Ramp Church Chattanooga, where I serve as lead pastor, we were in the middle of worship and I felt the nudging of the Spirit to interrupt worship and start laying hands on people. I wrestled in my mind a million reasons why I should not do this. I tried explaining to the Holy Spirit how we first needed to receive the offering and preach the Word, and then we can pray for the people. About that time the Holy Spirit spoke sternly to me, *"If you do not obey Me, then I will leave, and you can do this service by yourself."* He knew that would get me. I never want to go through the motions or minister from a vacant place. I quickly left my seat on the front row, made my way to the platform, and started releasing words of knowledge as He spoke them to me. I gave one about healing. I actually can't remember the exact word, but before I even finished it, I looked down and saw this little grandmother who had earlier entered into church, walking with the use of a cane. Suddenly, she threw down the cane and marched back and forth, totally healed. Still to this day she has not used her cane again. What if I had not been obedient to His voice and continued in the normal way of doing things? In this new move, religious devils will be driven out.

> *Afterward Jesus findeth him in the temple, and said unto him, Behold, thou art made whole: sin no more, lest a worse thing come unto thee. The man departed, and told the Jews that it was Jesus, which had made him whole* (John 5:14-15).

The impotent man who was healed experienced the *Triple Threat Anointing.* Jesus forgave his sins (salvation), healed his body (healing), and made him completely whole (deliverance). When you begin to walk in wholeness, not everyone will like it. In fact, they will want to shut it down, but you just keep walking in your freedom.

CHAPTER 7

---•◦•---

CHOICES

‖ Embracing or Rejecting ‖
the Movement

We all have been given free will. We have the ability to embrace or reject what God is doing on the earth. He will not force His will on us. Since the beginning of creation, when God created man, He gave every person the power of choice. Adam and Eve made the wrong choice when they ate the fruit of the tree of the knowledge of good and evil. Their choice opened the door for sin to enter the entire human race.

Choices have repercussions. Even as I am writing this, I am reminded of the fact that not everyone will embrace this coming wave of God. Not every church or believer will, or even wants to, experience the coming outpouring. There are churches that are filled with people every week, but have closed the door to the Holy Spirit. Those churches have, in essence, told God to move only on their terms. As long as He will move according to their schedule and within their set format, then they will accept His moving. God is through with being restricted by man. There is a remnant arising that will carry the glory of God. In fact, they are actively pursuing His glory.

There are so many stories in the Bible concerning choices. You can talk about Ruth and how she was faced with the option to leave Naomi, but every time she was given a choice, she made the steadfast decision that she was going to return with her.

> *And Ruth said, Intreat me not to leave thee, or to return from following after thee: for whither thou goest, I will go; and where thou lodgest, I will lodge: thy people shall be my people, and thy God my God: Where thou diest, will I die, and there will I be buried: the Lord do so to me, and more also, if ought but death part thee and me. When she saw that she was stedfastly minded to go with her, then she left speaking unto her* (Ruth 1:16-18).

The circumstances were that Naomi's husband and two sons had died, leaving two daughters-in-law faced with the decision to either go with Naomi to Bethlehem or return to their own hometown in Moab. They could move into the new, not knowing what the future held for them, or they could return to the old, which was familiar to them. Whenever God does a new thing, the most vocal criticism of it comes from the last move of God. People have the mindset of *this was how God did it for us and this is the only way He wants to move.* Sadly, it is often our own resistance that blocks the new flow of God in our lives. He passionately desires for us to embrace the new. We must remember He is a God who is constantly and consistently giving new beginnings. After all, He is Alpha and Omega, the Beginning and the End!

Orpah chose to go back to Moab, to the familiar, which was her old way of life, but Ruth stuck to Naomi and made the choice to embrace the new. The story of Ruth is a familiar Bible story, and it tells how in *the new* she met Boaz, who became her kinsman redeemer. Ruth ended up marrying Boaz and giving birth to a son named Obed, who had a son named Jesse, who had a son named David, whose lineage would bring forth the Messiah. Orpah, on the other hand, was believed to have brought forth a giant by the name of Goliath. Your choices do matter.

Are you willing to move out of your comfort zone? Are you ready to embrace the next move of God? Perhaps then the following Bible story in the Gospel of Mark will further persuade you to embrace the new. Chapter 5 of Mark begins with Jesus and the disciples coming into the country of the Gadarenes where they were immediately met by a man with an unclean spirit coming out from the tombs. This poor, wretched, and tormented man made his dwelling among the tombs. The Word of God said that no man could bind him, for he broke every chain. He was uncontrollable. Can you imagine today if a person possessed with a devil wreaked unfathomable havoc in the community you live in? Moreover, imagine the authorities did nothing because their former attempts were futile, and all they would say to you was, "There is nothing that we can do, for every time we try to arrest him, he just breaks out, so we have decided just to leave him alone."

Mark's Gospel records that this man could not be tamed. He cried night and day, cutting himself with stones until the moment he saw Jesus and ran to Him, begging Him not to torment him. Jesus spoke to the unclean spirit and commanded that it come out of the man. Jesus asked the spirit:

> *What is thy name? And he answered, saying, My name is Legion: for we are many. And he besought him much that he would not send them away out of the country* (Mark 5:9-10).

Notice that demonic spirits like certain territories. When you travel into different cities and regions, you can discern different spirits that are territorial spirits. In this story the evil spirits wanted permission to go into a herd of swine that was feeding nearby. Jesus allowed them to do so and the herd of swine violently ran down into a steep place into the sea and drowned about 2,000 pigs in the water.

> *And they that fed the swine fled, and told it in the city, and in the country. And they went out to see what it was that was done. And they come to Jesus, and see him that was possessed with the devil, and had the legion, sitting, and clothed, and in his right mind: and they were afraid. And they that saw it told them how it befell to him that was possessed with the devil, and also concerning the swine. And they began to pray him to depart out of their coasts* (Mark 5:14-17).

There are a few points that I would like for you to see in the above Scripture. The first point is that Jesus did not pacify the demons or try to make nice with the territorial spirits. He walked in authority and commanded them to come out of the man. Jesus cares more about the individual person than the great demonstrative act of power. He wanted to see the man set free from the demons that were tormenting him night and day.

The movement of the *Triple Threat Anointing* that God showed me is coming, which includes mass demonstrations of His power, is about those whose lives are being transformed. It was upon the individuals of the multitudes that He directed my focus! God desires that you allow Him to form *His* heart in you for individuals.

Second, the news was spread throughout all the city and country. They all came to see what was taking place. They all knew of the possessed man living among the tombs, and they heard that there was a Man who had entered their vicinity and set him free. They heard how He commanded the demons to come out of the man and into a herd of swine that drowned themselves into the sea. Can you imagine the astonished curiosity when the people of that region heard what had taken place in the maniac of Gadara? They came to see Jesus and he who was possessed with the devil, clothed and in his right mind and the Bible says, *"They were afraid"* (Mark 5:15). It has always baffled me that they were afraid of the power of God that set the man free. I wonder if they would have preferred him to remain as the wild man among the tombs?

> *Those who had seen it told the others what had happened to the demon-possessed man and the pigs. At first they were in awe—and then they were upset, upset over the drowned pigs. They demanded that Jesus leave and not come back* (Mark 5:16-17 MSG).

Gadara's citizens cared more about the pigs than the man who had been tormented for all of these years. They had a choice either to embrace the move of God or reject it. They chose to reject it and demanded that Jesus leave. He had interrupted their way of doing things. Who cared among them if people were possessed, as long as it did not disrupt their order of things? Every time I read this, my heart grieves because I can see the same thing paralleled in the Church today. Many churches profess to want God's presence, but they really only want His presence to the point that He doesn't make them uncomfortable. They've grown so accustomed to their way of doing church that if the Holy Spirit started moving, and they had not factored in a set time for it, they wouldn't know what to do. I truly believe that God is going to invade man's set structure of the way *we do* church. Get ready to see the moving of the Holy Spirit with signs following the believer. Get ready for the *Triple Threat Anointing* to fall in the churches!

As you read this book, you, like Ruth, are faced with a choice. God is saying, *"Will you embrace what I desire to do through you or will you reject it and settle for the norm?"* The Gadarenes saw His power, but counted the sacrifice of the lost financial gain from the drowned swine too much a cost to embrace what God desired to do there. What a sad choice that they made; they chose swine over the Son of God.

We must have the resolve to be a part of what God is doing and not the other way around. Too many of us are telling God to get in the midst of what *we* are doing. This is why being led by the Spirit of God is imperative. We cannot birth something in our flesh and ask God to bless it. Abraham, the friend of God, tried to persuade God into choosing Ishmael as the son of promise. We know that Ishmael was conceived by the plan of flesh and not the miraculous conception that God promised would come through Sarah.

God would not budge on choosing Isaac over Ishmael as the promised heir. The heir of Abraham's promise was to come through the womb of Sarah, even though she was past childbearing age. Wow! Meditate on this. This says to you and to me that every promise that has seemed as though is *too late or past due* is really right on time! It is not too late for your promise to come forth. Wait and see what God is doing. He is moving behind the scenes right now for you.

Let's move on to the story of the blind man who was healed in the Gospel of Mark. There were so many fascinating things about that particular miracle. The fact that Jesus used His spit to work this miracle stands out in this story, but the first thing to note is that Jesus took the blind man by the hand and led him out of the town of Bethsaida.

> *And he cometh to Bethsaida; and they bring a blind man unto him, and besought him to touch him. And he took the blind man by the hand, and led him out of the town; and when he had spit on his eyes, and put his hands upon him, he asked him if he saw ought* (Mark 8:22-23).

The reason that Jesus took him by the hand and led him out of the town of Bethsaida was because Jesus had cursed the city for seeing mighty wonders and still not repenting. He refused to do any more miracles there.

> *Then He began to denounce [the people in] the cities in which most of His miracles were done, because they did not repent [and change their hearts and lives]. "Woe (judgment is coming) to you, Chorazin! Woe to you, Bethsaida! For if the miracles done in you had been done in Tyre and Sidon [cities of the Gentiles], they would have repented long ago in sackcloth and ashes [their hearts would have been changed and they would have expressed sorrow for their sin and rebellion against God]. Nevertheless I say to you, it will be more tolerable for [the pagan cities of] Tyre and Sidon on the day of judgment than for you. And you, Capernaum, are you to be exalted to heaven [for your apathy and unresponsiveness]? You will descend to Hades (the realm of the dead); for if the miracles done in you had been done in Sodom, it would have remained until this day. But I say to you, it will be more tolerable for the land of Sodom on the day of judgment, than for you"* (Matthew 11:20-24 AMP).

Like these cities and the country of the Gadarenes we have a choice. We can embrace the move of God in our lives, churches, and this generation, or we can reject it. What is your choice?

CHAPTER 8

THE NEW TESTAMENT CHURCH

‖ FOLLOWING JESUS IN ‖ THE TRIPLE THREAT

The followers of Jesus Christ had suffered the greatest trauma that anyone could ever experience after He was crucified on the cross. They could not comprehend the events that had just taken place in Jerusalem. They believed Jesus had come to build His kingdom upon the earth. They had waited for Him to overthrow the Roman Empire, freeing their nation from the yoke of oppression, and even though they had watched and waited, it never happened. Their new reality was that it would never happen. The One whom they had followed for three and a half years was now dead, and not only was He dead, but He was buried in a tomb and a massive stone sealed it.

All they had hoped for and imagined would now never take place. They couldn't wrap their minds around all of it. They were devastated and felt lost. Where were they to go? What were they to do? They had no purpose.

Unfortunately, they suffered greatly because they had not received the revelation Christ so diligently sought to get over to them. He had told them He would suffer and die. Yet they refused to receive it because it did not line up with their agenda for Jesus; they had written their own story. As I reflect upon the feelings of the early believers, I can't help but reflect upon my own life. Is there anything God has tried to get over to me and I'm just not getting it because I've written my own story?

I always humanize the people I am studying, imagining what they must have felt or thought in the midst of their encounters or trials and relating it to myself. Whenever I get to the crucifixion, I not only meditate upon the suffering of Christ when He paid the cost of redemption for the whole world, but I also think about the pain His followers experienced. I believe I would have felt the same as them. So many of them had given up everything in order to follow Him.

Mary Magdalene is one of my favorites. According to all four Gospels, she was a witness to the death, burial, and resurrection of Jesus. The Bible tells us that Mary was from the town of Magdala, giving the reason for her surname, Magdalene. Many theologians believe that she had been a prostitute before she met Jesus. Even though the Bible doesn't unequivocally state that Mary Magdalene had been a prostitute, the fact was that Magdala, where many fishermen frequently visited, was rumored to be a town that promoted prostitution. Moreover, she was a woman with resources (see Luke 8:3). In that time, it was very uncommon for unmarried women to have finances; therefore, the conclusion was that she probably had been a prostitute.

> *Soon afterwards he went on through cities and villages, proclaiming and bringing the good news of the kingdom of God. The twelve were with him, as well as some women who had been cured of evil spirits and infirmities: Mary, called Magdalene, from whom seven demons had gone out, and Joanna, the wife of Herod's steward Chuza, and Susanna, and many others, who provided for them out of their resources* (Luke 8:1-3 NRSV).

In the day in which she lived, unmarried women were thought of in scandalous terms and were not accepted like they are today, especially if they were possessed with seven devils! She was rejected, used, and probably isolated until she encountered Jesus who cast those seven demons out of her. He set her free from a lifetime of hurt and torment. She had finally found her purpose, and life took on new meaning for her. She discovered God's love for her. No longer was she tormented; no longer was she used by men. From that point on, she invested everything into following Jesus.

I can't even imagine the pain that she felt as she stood watching as Jesus was beaten until He was unrecognizable. Her heart must have been in a million pieces as she witnessed the ordeal playing out before her eyes. No doubt she wailed in pain, pleading for them to stop hurting the Son of God. The despair she must have felt as she saw Him lifted up on a cross, nails in His hands and feet. There He hung, and then it was over. Jesus was dead. All of her dreams seemed to die with Him. Her heart and mind were in turmoil. Everything she believed was called into question. The thoughts that she must have wrestled with in her mind—*Was it all not true? Do I go back to my old life? Where are You, God? Why didn't You save Him? Why did He not come off the cross and demonstrate His power?*

Even in the state of pure emotional, mental, and even physical exhaustion from the traumatic ordeal that she had lived through, her love for Jesus pushed her to still get up. Early that Sunday morning she went to the tomb where Jesus had been buried, in order to bring spices to care for the corpse of the One who had changed her life. As she arrived, while it was still dark, she experienced a miracle, which she never expected.

Let me stop here a moment and say to you that the circumstances that you are facing may appear very dark, but know this—even in the darkest of nights, your God is moving for you. I remind you that God works the night-shift! Your God moves when it looks as though nothing is happening. You are about to experience a third-day resurrection. Dead things are going to come to life. Dead dreams, dead promises, and dead relationships are coming back to life!

Mary Magdalene arrived before the breaking of day, expecting to find a sealed tomb with guards securing it, but instead she saw the massive stone had been rolled away. She ran to tell Peter and John that *"They have taken away the Lord out of the sepulchre, and we know not where they have laid him"* (John 20:2).

Mary's emotions were in an upheaval. She not only was mourning the loss of her Lord, but now they had taken His corpse from the tomb. She could not even grieve, as was the custom. She must have been thinking, *Why? What is next?*

> *But Mary stood without at the sepulchre weeping: and as she wept, she stooped down, and looked into the sepulchre, and seeth two angels in white sitting, the one at the head, and the other at the feet, where the body of Jesus had lain. And they say unto her, Woman, why weepest thou? She saith unto them, Because they have taken away my Lord, and I know not where they have laid him. And when she had thus said, she turned herself*

back, and saw Jesus standing, and knew not that it was Jesus. Jesus saith unto her, Woman, why weepest thou? whom seekest thou? She, supposing him to be the gardener, saith unto him, Sir, if thou have borne him hence, tell me where thou hast laid him, and I will take him away. Jesus saith unto her, Mary. She turned herself, and saith unto him, Rabboni; which is to say, Master. Jesus saith unto her, Touch me not; for I am not yet ascended to my Father: but go to my brethren, and say unto them, I ascend unto my Father, and your Father; and to my God, and your God (John 20:11-17).

Mary was the first person to see Jesus after the resurrection. In an instant, she went from the darkest hour of her life to the brightest moment of joy that she had ever experienced. And let me say to you that like God did for Mary, He can *suddenly* turn your worst tragedy into your greatest triumph! Some of you have had your dreams crushed. You have cried tears of mourning, but I hear the Spirit of the Lord say, *"You are going from mourning to morning!"* God is breaking through the darkness to release a miracle you could not even dream or imagine. He is able to do it, and I believe He is doing it right now! Remember, God works even in the night season. When you cannot see Him, He is still there, working for your good.

Then the same day at evening, being the first day
of the week, when the doors were shut where the
disciples were assembled for fear of the Jews, came
Jesus and stood in the midst, and saith unto them,
Peace be unto you (John 20:19).

The disciples had gathered together and were hiding behind locked doors because of fear of the Jews. They saw what the Jews did to Jesus; they knew what they were capable of doing. And while they were hiding in fear, Jesus came to them. The enemy thought he had them locked in fear, shrinking in the corner, afraid of what would happen, but Jesus came and unlocked them from the chain of fear. He exchanged their fear for peace.

Then said Jesus to them again, Peace be unto you:
as my Father hath sent me, even so send I you.
And when he had said this, he breathed on them,
and saith unto them, Receive ye the Holy Ghost
(John 20:21-22).

Jesus then commissioned them and sent them forth to do the works of the Father, even as Christ had been sent to the earth. They, like Christ, were sent forth, possessing an apostolic mandate to represent Jesus on the earth. He empowered them as He breathed on them.

The Greek word translated *breathed* is the Greek verb *emphusaø*, meaning "to blow at or on; to breathe on." Jesus was not only using this act as a representation of the Spirit but also as a means to impart new life into His disciples with a new impartation of the Holy Spirit. He said, *"Receive ye the Holy Ghost."* The Greek word translated *ghost* is the word *pneuma,* meaning "a current of air that is breath (blast) or a breeze (divine); God's and Christ's Spirit, the Holy Spirit."

> *And the Lord God formed man of the dust of the ground, and breathed into his nostrils the breath of life; and man became a living soul* (Genesis 2:7).

When God breathes on your situation, things begin to change. In the verses that were just discussed, God was breathing a wind of impartation and life. One of my favorite examples of God breathing is found in the Book of Exodus. God miraculously delivered the Israelites from Egyptian bondage. He raised Moses up as a deliverer to lead the Hebrew people out of oppression and into freedom. God displayed His power to Pharaoh, the Egyptians, and to the Israelites while they were still in Egypt. He mightily demonstrated His power by the plagues that caused Pharaoh to finally let God's people go. However, God told Moses that Pharaoh's heart would be hardened and he would try to enslave the Israelites once again, but not to fear because God would bring their deliverance to a crescendo of sorts.

For Pharaoh will say of the children of Israel,
They are entangled in the land, the wilderness
hath shut them in. And I will harden Pharaoh's
heart, that he shall follow after them; and I will
be honoured upon Pharaoh, and upon all his
host; that the Egyptians may know that I am the
Lord. And they did so (Exodus 14:3-4).

The Israelites were trapped having the Red Sea in front of them and Pharaoh's army quickly coming behind them. In other words, they were *between the devil and the deep blue sea!* They instinctively became upset with Moses. They complained, "Why did you bring us to the wilderness to die? It would have been better for us to have died in Egypt." What they did not understand was that God was turning their obstacle into their greatest miracle. (I decree right now that the obstacles in your life are turning into your greatest miracles!)

And Moses stretched out his hand over the sea;
and the Lord caused the sea to go back by a
strong east wind all that night, and made the sea
dry land, and the waters were divided. And the
children of Israel went into the midst of the sea
upon the dry ground: and the waters were a wall
unto them on their right hand, and on their left
(Exodus 14:21-22).

God caused the sea to go back by a strong east "wind." When God breathes into a situation, life is given, things begin to happen, and everything changes. When Jesus breathed on the disciples, there was an impartation of new life given to them. A mantle was placed on them, and they were sent forth with an apostolic mandate to build the kingdom of God.

The word translated *wind* is the Hebrew word *ruach,* meaning "wind; by resemblance (breath) that is a sensible (or even violent) exaltation; figuratively (life)."

And he said unto them, Go ye into all the world, and preach the gospel to every creature. He that believeth and is baptized shall be saved; but he that believeth not shall be damned. And these signs shall follow them that believe; In my name shall they cast out devils; they shall speak with new tongues; they shall take up serpents; and if they drink any deadly thing, it shall not hurt them; they shall lay hands on the sick, and they shall recover. So then after the Lord had spoken unto them, he was received up into heaven, and sat on the right hand of God. And they went forth, and preached every where, the Lord working with them, and confirming the word with signs following. Amen (Mark 16:15-20).

Jesus said, *"signs shall follow them that believe."* If you are a believer in Jesus and the finished work He did on the cross, signs should be following you. You have authority through the name of Jesus and the Holy Spirit working through you. Your purpose is to "preach the Gospel," "cast out devils," and to "heal the sick." Here in the Great Commission, Jesus laid out the principles for the *Triple Threat Anointing* that He showed to me in my dream. This is not the great suggestion! No, it is the Great Commission. A commission is an authoritative order. The word *commission* is defined as "the act of committing or entrusting a person, group, etc., with supervisory power or authority; an authoritative order, charge, or direction."[1]

I started this chapter writing about Mary Magdalene and her story, but let's take a look at another one of the central characters God used in establishing the New Testament church. His name was Simon; the Lord would later change his name to Peter. Most would consider him the most unlikely of candidates to be front and center of the beginnings of the greatest religious movement the world has ever known.

Peter lived in Capernaum, a town near the Sea of Galilee. He and his brother, Andrew, grew up in a fishing village and were born into a family of fishermen. It was an obvious choice for them to go into the family occupation, and that is just what they did. They partnered with two other brothers, James and John, in their fishing business. Though they were busy business owners, and probably somewhat gruff fishermen, they were still intrigued by the things of God as evidenced by their traveling to the Jordan River to hear John the Baptist preach his message of "Repent, for the kingdom of God is at hand!"

It was around that time they heard the news spreading around Galilee—a dynamic teacher and a miracle worker was coming to town. Imagine their great excitement and anticipation. They, being Jewish, knew all the prophecies of the coming Messiah. First and foremost in their thoughts must have been, *Is this Him?*

When Simon first met Jesus, he was married with a family. He owned a fishing business and was a hard worker, but he knew there was something more. There was a longing in his heart for something greater. When Simon first encountered Jesus, his mother-in-law was sick with a fever. They asked Jesus to come and heal her. Jesus entered into Simon's house and rebuked the fever, and his wife's mother was totally healed. In that moment, he witnessed firsthand the power and authority that Jesus possessed. However, this miracle was not what caught the heart of Simon. It was a later event that changed the trajectory of Simon's life.

I believe that Simon, like a lot of people today, received the validation of his identity through his career. He was a business owner; that's who he was. And he was good at it. In fact, it was what Peter returned to after the crucifixion and resurrection. It was what he knew. He was comfortable with it. When he was under pressure, fishing was what he chose as an escape. He needed an escape because his world had been turned upside down by the Lord's death. However, Jesus was about to interrupt what Simon thought he wanted and reveal God's destiny for his life. He was about to experience *the more* that God had for him.

Why is it that we often settle for the mundane when God is calling us to more? We are not on this earth to live a nice, normal life, merely existing until we die. Out of all the generations, before and after, God chose us to be born at this time, in this generation. We are not here taking up space; we are here to unlock Heaven on earth. We have the keys to the kingdom. God desires that we live in the *more* zone. More of God, the Father. More of Jesus, the Son. More of the Holy Ghost and power. We never get to a place in God where He is finished revealing Himself to us. He always has more.

This was the case with Simon. He was about to experience *the more*. One day, Jesus saw two empty boats, and the fishermen were washing their nets. Out of all the boats on the Sea of Galilee, Jesus stepped into Simon's boat. He instructed him to thrust out a little from the land. As he did, Jesus sat down and started teaching the people from the boat. Simon's boat was his gift to God. In a manner of speaking, it was a seed to build a platform for the Gospel to be preached. Whenever a seed is sown into good ground you can always expect a harvest from that seed. Giving is likened unto sowing a seed.

It is thrilling to me that Jesus chose to partner with Simon and Andrew. We sometimes look at this story and determine that Jesus needed a boat in order to teach the people. It is true that Jesus used the boat as a platform for the Word to be taught, but He did not need it. My point is this—Jesus could have walked on the water to preach His message, but He chose to use what Simon and Andrew had in order to release the fullness of God's plan in their life. I am so thankful that God has chosen to partner with us to accomplish His purpose.

After Jesus was finished teaching, He gave Simon an unusual instruction, *"Launch out into the deep, and let down your nets for a draught"* (Luke 5:4). I wonder if Simon was thinking to himself, *I am the professional fisherman here. You are the teacher. You do your job and I will do mine.* Instead, though, Simon answered Him by stating his current circumstances, saying, *"Master, we have toiled all the night, and have taken nothing"* (Luke 5:5). If he had stopped there, Simon might not have ever experienced his true destiny. Many people are at the edge of breakthrough, but they refuse to move past their current circumstances. Could it be that you, like Simon, are facing insurmountable odds against you? Have you been toiling all night and caught nothing? Have you been washing your nets, saying, "It's over. That didn't work out." I hear God saying something different to you. He is saying, *"I have something better for you!"*

Back to Simon—no, Simon did not stop with his current dilemma of "We tried all night. It's over." He went on to say a word that changed his life, a word God loves, seeing that He recorded it so many times in Scripture, always in connection with insurmountable odds. That word is *nevertheless.* Sometimes you have to look at your situation and say, "Nevertheless!" I know it looks hopeless, but nevertheless. I know I tried before, but nevertheless. Start speaking *nevertheless* to your crisis right now!

Simon said to Jesus, *"Nevertheless at thy word I will let down the net"* (Luke 5:5). This is *the key* to your breakthrough—believe His Word to you. Find a promise from the Bible to stand on. One prophetic Word from God can shift everything in your life. Whenever God gives you a prophetic instruction, obey what He tells you to do. It may seem illogical, people may not understand it, but it doesn't matter whether they understand it or not. They are not the one needing a breakthrough. You are! That's why you must believe His Word, obey His voice, and receive your breakthrough.

It was pretty illogical for Joshua and the children of Israel to march around Jericho in complete silence one time a day for six days, then seven times on the seventh day. They were told on the seventh day and the seventh time around, when they hear the blast of the horn, to lift up a shout. They had a prophetic promise that the wall would fall down flat and they would take the city.

It did not make sense in the natural, but that is exactly what happened. It looked absurd for King Jehoshaphat of Judah to send the singers out to sing praises when three armies were coming to destroy them. Yet this is what happened, and God gave them complete victory. It also looked foolish when David refused King Saul's armor in favor of his slingshot and five smooth stones. Amazingly, the slingshot and stones was his weapon of choice against the mighty giant warrior, Goliath. He miraculously hit the giant in his forehead and Goliath fell to the ground. David cut off that giant's head. All three of these great feats were accomplished through radical obedience.

You may be saying to yourself, *That is great that it worked for them in the Bible, but it won't work for me.* Don't believe satan's lie! Their God is your God. He is still the same yesterday, today, and forever. He is no respecter of persons. If you will listen for His instructions and obey Him with radical obedience, then you, too, will receive everything that God has promised you. When Simon obeyed the instruction of Jesus, he caught so many fish that the nets broke. Let me interject here— if you have a business, the answer to your business is in His Word. Moreover, the answer to your ministry is in His Word. Finally, the answer to every one of life's questions is found in the Word and your obedience to His instruction. Get radical, believe with audacious faith.

God knows exactly how to reach us and speak our language. For Simon, Jesus reached him through instruction for his business. For you, it might be through your children, your marriage, or through your profession. Whatever your language is, God knows how to speak it to reach you. He knows everything about you. He also knows all about that lost loved one for whom you are praying. Don't give up! Keep praying. He knows their language, too.

I heard a story about Reverend Billy Graham. He decided to go minister on the streets with Arthur Blessitt, the preacher who has carried the cross all over the world. Being as recognizable as Billy Graham was caused a great security concern. They decided that Billy Graham would wear sunglasses and a baseball hat and that would disguise him enough to go. As Reverend Graham was ministering to one man and telling him all about Jesus, the man interrupted and said he was not interested in hearing what he had to say. He further said there was only one minister he would listen to and that was Billy Graham. Reverend Graham pulled off his glasses and his hat and said, "God sent me to you today. Today is your day." This story proves my point—God knows exactly what it takes to reach you.

There is an apostle friend of mine from the United Kingdom who is incredibly accurate when he moves in the gift of the word of knowledge. He was flying back to London after ministering in the US and had a layover in

Chicago. He received a word of knowledge for a woman who was standing in line in front of him at the ticket counter. The Lord told him to tell her to leave her place in line now and run to Terminal 3, Concourse D, and there she would find her brother whom she hadn't seen in 29 years. The woman was on the phone speaking in another language when the word came to him. He had to interrupt this woman's phone call, and her a stranger to him, to give her this word. He was radically obedient. The woman ran and went to where he had directed her. Some time later, she returned to the terminal where Apostle Oscar waited, but she was not alone. She came screaming with joy along with her brother, Dennis. They began to ask questions and he was able to lead them to Christ. God knew her language and what it would take to reach both her and her brother.

When Simon let down his net, he and his partners caught so many fish that their nets broke and the boats began to sink under the weight of all the fish. When they made it to shore, Simon fell to his knees. He first responded with fear, recognizing that he was sinful, but Jesus passed beyond that because He was after Simon's heart. Jesus released his true destiny that day when He told him that he would be a "fisher of men." Jesus said, *"Fear not; from henceforth thou shalt catch men. And when they had brought their ships to land, they forsook all, and followed him"* (Luke 5:10-11). And that day, Simon, his brother Andrew, and their business partners

James and John were so greatly impacted that they forsook everything and followed Jesus.

Peter was known for running off at the mouth, but he had a heart after Jesus. He could be, at times, impulsive. He was the only man other than Jesus who ever walked on the water. Don't focus on the fact that he took his eyes off of Jesus and onto the storm and then began to sink. The focus should be that he stepped out of the boat and walked on water. He did it! The other disciples never knew the thrill of walking on water, but Peter knew it. He left the other disciples behind, debating whether Jesus was a ghost or not. Peter took action. The other disciples will never know if they could have walked on the water, for they were too scared to try.

Some of you reading this may be afraid to try something new. When I was younger, I only wanted to participate in activities that I felt confident doing. I was too afraid that I would look foolish if I tried something new. I regret being trapped in the boat of fear. I wish that I had been a little more like Peter, refusing to let fear dictate to me to stay in the boat.

I think it is important to speak of not only Peter's faith, but also of the time his faith was weak. Peter has been the most favorite among all the disciples because many can identify with him. One moment he was as bold as the lion, and the next moment he was weak. The time of his weak faith happened later after he had walked on water. Peter told Jesus how he would never deny Him. I believe in his heart he meant it when he gave his absolute affirmation that he would never forsake the Lord. Nonetheless, we know that he did just that as Jesus prophesied he would do. Peter did, indeed, deny Him three times before the rooster crowed. However, in a beautiful picture of the mercy of God and the love Jesus had for Peter, he was set apart by name from the other disciples when the angel spoke to the women at the tomb. In other words, God had sent a heavenly messenger to make sure that Peter knew that he was still included among the disciples, and complete restoration was his portion even after his denial.

> *But go your way, tell his disciples and Peter that he goeth before you into Galilee: there shall ye see him, as he said unto you* (Mark 16:7).

Like Peter, you may have blown it. It is not too late to get back up. Do not allow the enemy to keep you bound to condemnation. There is still breath in your body, and God has a plan for you. The Spirit of the Lord would have me to say to you, "It is not over." God wants to partner with you and commission you into His purpose for your life. You may be washing your nets saying, "I tried. It just didn't work." However, right now God is releasing a "nevertheless" miracle to you. He is calling you to walk in this *Triple Threat Anointing.*

NOTE

1. Dictionary.com, s.v. "Commission," https://www .dictionary.com/browse/commission.

CHAPTER 9

DEMONSTRATION OF POWER

The Triple Threat, Then and Now

The study of church history and prior movements reveals two predominant commonalities. First, the movements always started with individuals who were hungry for more of God. They refused to stay in the confines of religion. Second, *prayer birthed every move of God*. I would also elaborate here that prayer also sustained every move of God.

I have a prayer room located over the garage in our house. I call it my "Upper Room." In this room, I have a prayer wall and I post Scriptures, prayer requests, and other things that I bring before the Lord. The bedroom of my daughter, Giuliana, is located next to our garage and is under the prayer room as well. One day, while I was spending time with the Lord in prayer, lying prostrate before Him, my attention was drawn to the door that was slowly opening. A little face peeped around the door. It was little Giuliana. My immediate response was to tell her that Daddy was busy, she should go play, and Daddy would be down in a little bit. As I opened my mouth to speak those words, I heard the Holy Spirit rebuke me. He said to me, *"Your daughter needs to see her father praying. I want her to be familiar with My presence."* So instead of telling her to go away, I invited her to come in and pray with me.

I continued lying on the floor and weeping before the Lord because the presence of God charged the atmosphere. Giuliana came and lay beside me and she, too, began to weep in the Lord's presence. He was doing a special work in her life, and I knew it. My first thought was that it was so sweet of her to imitate me, but the Lord said, *"She is not imitating you. I am putting My hand upon her. She will be filled with the Holy Ghost and be given her prayer language today."* He went on to say, *"Lay your hands on her now and explain to her what is happening to her."* As I did, I felt fire flow from my hands, and immediately she began to speak with other tongues. We both stayed for hours praying and worshiping the Lord.

As I write now, the Holy Spirit is speaking to me on the importance of prayer. He is saying that we must pray like never before. Sometimes, when we hear of a third great awakening or an outpouring that is coming, we fall into the trap of believing that all we have to do is wait it out. We succumb to the lackadaisical outlook that God will move whenever He feels like it. Waiting on God does not mean being lazy. It means that we are actively preparing for what God has promised. He has sent us an invitation to partner with the Holy Spirit and to become His vessels, releasing the glory of the Lord upon the earth. Wow, did that hit your spirit? The God of the universe wants to use us to represent Him!

This is not the time for us to be apathetic in our daily pursuit of Him. No! He is imploring us, as sons and daughters, to cry out to Him for a movement of His Spirit, *"for tremendous power is released through the passionate, heartfelt prayer of a godly believer!"* (James 5:16 TPT). There must be persistence in prayer. Prayer should never be minimized as a last-ditch effort when we are in trouble and only practiced when our circumstances look dire. It should be our lifeline to God. It is where intimacy is birthed with the Father. There is nothing that can be a replacement for our life of prayer. We must guard our times of prayer at all cost.

> *One day Jesus told his disciples a story to show that they should always pray and never give up. "There was a judge in a certain city," he said, "who neither feared God nor cared about people. A widow of that city came to him repeatedly,*

saying, 'Give me justice in this dispute with my enemy.' The judge ignored her for a while, but finally he said to himself, 'I don't fear God or care about people, but this woman is driving me crazy. I'm going to see that she gets justice, because she is wearing me out with her constant requests!'"

Then the Lord said, "Learn a lesson from this unjust judge. Even he rendered a just decision in the end. So don't you think God will surely give justice to his chosen people who cry out to him day and night? Will he keep putting them off? I tell you, he will grant justice to them quickly! But when the Son of Man returns, how many will he find on the earth who have faith?" (Luke 18:1-8 NLT)

Jesus used this parable to teach His disciples that God rewards persistent prayer. Some people believe that if they ask once that should be sufficient, but that's not always the case! It is an irresponsible position to think that if God wants it to happen then it will, and if He doesn't then it won't. God has entrusted to us the power to release Heaven to earth. The method that we use to bring His will on the earth is through the vehicle of prayer.

Yes, God hears your request the first time you pray, but He desires for you to contend in prayer. There is a work that He is doing inside of you as you seek after Him. You are learning to be utterly dependent upon Him alone. God is preparing you for the manifestation of your request. The bride is now being made ready to carry this *Triple Threat Anointing* and to steward the harvest that comes with this new movement.

There is much to ascertain from the prayer life of Jesus, while He walked the earth as Man. The Bible paints the picture of Him as a Man of prayer who frequently withdrew Himself from others to pray.

> *After the crowds dispersed, Jesus went up into the hills to pray. And as night fell he was there praying alone with God* (Matthew 14:23 TPT).
>
> *The next morning, Jesus got up long before daylight, left the house while it was dark, and made his way to a secluded place to give himself to prayer* (Mark 1:35 TPT).
>
> *However, the report went around concerning Him all the more; and great multitudes came together to hear, and to be healed by Him of their infirmities. So He Himself often withdrew into the wilderness and prayed* (Luke 5:15-16 NKJV).
>
> *Now it came to pass in those days that He went out to the mountain to pray, and continued all night in prayer to God* (Luke 6:12 NKJV).

The above verses were just a *few* of Scriptures that described the prayer life of Jesus. Notice what it says— Jesus, *"continued all night in prayer to God."* It was during those times of prayer, as Jesus communed with the Father, that He was supercharged to fulfill the will of His heavenly Father.

I can't help but wonder what would happen if every Christian began to pray and to ask God to pour out His Spirit. What would happen if all believers asked the Lord to use them as His vessel to accomplish His will on the earth? I believe that we would see a radical change in every town, village, city, state, province, and nation—every corner of the earth.

Do you believe that God answers prayer? I know that He does. Jesus desired to prove to the public that God does, indeed, hear and answer prayer. He illustrated this at the tomb of His friend, Lazarus. In the natural, it seemed like a very inopportune time to demonstrate the power of prayer; however, Jesus saw this moment as the perfect time to show forth the glory of God. He used this crisis to communicate that God hears and answers prayer. He further divulged that prayer is the key to demonstrating the power of God to the world.

> So they rolled away the heavy stone. Jesus gazed into heaven and said, "Father, thank you that you have heard my prayer, for you listen to every word I speak. Now, so that these who stand here with me will believe that you have sent me to the earth as your messenger, I will use the power you have given me" (John 11:41-42 TPT).

Furthermore, the Bible says that Jesus stood before the tomb and cried with a loud voice, saying, *"Lazarus come forth,"* and Lazarus, bound with the garments of death, came out of the tomb. Jesus' prayer had been heard, which became a message for all to know that God will take the painful experiences of life to show forth His glory.

Remember that Jesus laid aside His God-attributes and walked as all Man upon this earth. In other words, He did the works He did because He was empowered by the Spirit of God and not because He was God. That means we can do the same! He laid aside His God-attributes (omnipotent, omniscient, and omnipresent) and, in fact, had to pray to the Father to have them restored (see John 17:4-5 AMP). Listen! He was the same as you and me in the respect that He needed the Holy Spirit. The power that flowed through Him was given through the Holy Spirit, as a result of prayer and obedience. You and I have the same Spirit that lives and dwells inside of us. We must tap into His power through relationship with Him.

One day after the disciples observed Jesus praying, they asked Him to teach them to pray. They desired to learn to pray in the same manner that He did. They rightly concluded that His disciplined prayer life and constant communication with the Father was the source of His power and the supernatural miracles that He worked.

Once Jesus was in a certain place praying. As he finished, one of his disciples came to him and said, "Lord, teach us to pray, just as John taught his disciples" (Luke 11:1 NLT).

It is very significant that the disciples asked Him to teach them to pray. They did not ask Him how to work miracles, neither did they ask Him how to multiply bread and fish, nor did they even ask how to raise the dead. They grasped the truth that all of these supernatural demonstrative acts were intertwined with His consecration in prayer. If we will grab hold of this revelation and put it into action in our lives, then we too will be used to turn our world upside down with the message of the Gospel.

> One of these days some simple soul will pick
> up the Book of God, read it, *and believe it.*
> Then the rest of us will be embarrassed.[1]

I was baptized with the Holy Ghost and received my prayer language at age four. After that, I started having nightly prayer meetings in my little bedroom. I sang at the top of my lungs in worship to the Lord. I gave Him a concert for an audience of One. I was just as loud then as I am now. Thankfully, my parents encouraged me to continue in prayer and worship rather than telling me to turn down the music. In those times of worship, long before my feet ever hit a real platform, God was building me a platform in the secret place with Him. He was preparing me for pleasing Him rather than people.

I can vividly remember kneeling beside the chair in my room and knowing that He was in there with me. Sometimes, I was afraid to look up, not knowing what I might see because His glory was there. It was not a fear of terror, but rather a fear of reverence. Every night, I would put on accompaniment tracks and sing to Him. He was and still is the best audience. He loved every song I sang; even the notes that weren't quite right, He still enjoyed it. Early on, I learned the secret to His presence was through worship.

Then I would start praying. I asked Him every night for the same thing: "God, flow through me and use me to tell people about You." At the time, I did not realize that there would be a cost. I was just so in love with Him that I desperately wanted to be used of Him. He took my little boy prayers seriously and *has done and is presently doing* just as I asked of Him so many years ago. It was during these early years that a lifestyle of prayer and worship was developed in me. I had been marked by the power of prayer.

In the coming movement, God's people will begin to demonstrate His power in unexpected places. Yes, we will see God move greatly in our churches, revival centers, and prayer houses, but He will also show forth His power outside the four walls of the church. He will move through technology, social media, books, recordings, and other innovative ways. God's people will see His power in action flowing through them in the *Triple Threat Anointing*. God is not restricted to our places of worship. It will be His people who will be the movement and carry His glory, for it pleases the Lord to bless His children and to move through them. Everywhere His children shall go, the *Triple Threat Anointing* will also go because the Holy Spirit is living on the inside of His people.

God is raising up bold believers who are unafraid of exhibiting God's power to the world. In fact, as I have stated in previous chapters, the *dunamis* power, or dynamite power, will not be contained. I believe His people will go to the grocery store or to a restaurant or anywhere else that people gather, and God will move like we have never seen before. Believers must yield themselves to Him and partner with the Holy Spirit in order to see this movement. The gifts of the Spirit in the early Church were in operation wherever believers went, whether it was in the marketplace or in the Temple or in the town square. The world is on the cusp of seeing Him move again through His Church!

Let me be clear—I am not saying that God is not currently moving, which would be foolish because He is moving. Every day souls are saved, the sick are healed, and the captives are delivered. What I saw, though, was that miracles would become the new standard rather than an occasional occurrence.

Luke recorded the story of the apostle Paul's time in Athens, Greece (see Acts 17:15-34). Paul was grieved at the idol worship that dominated the city. He preached the resurrection of Jesus Christ in the synagogue and also in the marketplace. He impressed some of the Greeks, and they brought him to a meeting at the Areopagus (Mars Hill), the high court of Athens. He preached what today is referred to as the "Areopagus Sermon." In it, Paul boldly confronted their pagan worship and the ignorance in making an altar to worship an "unknown god." He delivered what some would say to be one of the most eloquent presentations of the Gospel. Although his teaching was well spoken, it did not produce exceptional results. (There is still much debate and differing opinions on the *approach* he used to minister in Athens.)

After Paul left Athens, he went to Corinth, and there his method of delivery was different than it was on Mars Hill:

And I, brethren, when I came to you, did not come with excellence of speech or of wisdom declaring to you the testimony of God. For I determined not to know anything among you except Jesus Christ and Him crucified. I was with you in weakness, in fear, and in much trembling. And my speech and my preaching were not with persuasive words of human wisdom, but in demonstration of the Spirit and of power, that your faith should not be in the wisdom of men but in the power of God (1 Corinthians 2:1-5 NKJV).

The word *demonstration,* as used in the above Scriptural passage, was translated from the Greek word *apodeixsis,* which means "a making manifest, a showing forth," and "a demonstration." After his experience in Athens, Paul was going to make sure the next city, Corinth, was impacted with a demonstration of God's power. He knew that if he wanted to birth a move of God in this territory, it would require him to not only preach but to also show forth God's power. Take note here—the movement that is coming will not be filled with enticing words and man's wisdom, but it will be full of the Holy Ghost and demonstrations of His power!

After Corinth, the apostle Paul was led to evangelize Ephesus (see Acts 19). Ephesus was the center of travel and commerce because of its location on the Aegean Sea. The Aegean Sea is located with the Greek peninsula on the west and Asia Minor on the east. It was one of the greatest seaports of the ancient world.

Ephesus was also the epicenter of worship to Artemis, the Greek goddess of hunting, wildlife, and chastity. She was considered the protectress of women during childbirth. This false goddess was worshiped throughout the world and was known by the Greeks as

Artemis and by the Romans as Diana. Her temple was considered one of the great wonders of the world and it was located in Ephesus. If there was ever any place that needed to see God's power demonstrated, it was Ephesus. Paul knew that he could never win the people there to Christ with poetic words. He knew he needed to demonstrate the power of God through the name of Jesus, and that was exactly what He did. He moved in the *Triple Threat Anointing!*

And God wrought special miracles by the hands of Paul: so that from his body were brought unto the sick handkerchiefs or aprons, and the diseases departed from them, and the evil spirits went out of them (Acts 19:11-12).

God did extraordinary miracles through Paul in Ephesus. The *Triple Threat Anointing* flowed through Paul, and a great move of God spread throughout Ephesus.

The *Triple Threat Anointing* was scripturally proven to have been active in the move of God that occurred under the leadership of Paul in the city of Ephesus:

1. Healing—the *"sick"* were healed and *"diseases departed."*
2. Deliverance—"evil spirits went out of them."
3. Salvation—*"many...believed"* (Acts 19:18).

Many believers publicly confessed their sins and disclosed their secrets. Large numbers of those who had been practicing magic took all of their books and scrolls of spells and incantations and publicly burned them. When the value of all the books and scrolls was calculated, it all came to several million dollars. The power of God caused the word to spread, and the people were greatly impacted (Acts 19:18-20 TPT).

As a result of the demonstration of the power of God and the combination of the *Triple Threat Anointing*, the Word of God spread throughout the world, and the people were forever impacted.

NOTE

1. Leonard Ravenhill, *Why Revival Tarries* (Bloomington, MN: Bethany House Publishers, 1987), 71.

———■·○·■———

CHAPTER 10

THE HOLY GHOST EFFECT

‖ THE UNSTOPPABLE MOVEMENT ‖

I have titled this chapter "The Holy Ghost Effect," because when the Holy Ghost is at work, everything changes. It is imperative for you to receive the revelation that the same miraculous works that Jesus did while He walked as Man upon this earth, He still does *through the power of the Holy Spirit*, only He uses His Church to do them, meaning He has multiplied His ministry, doing exploits in an even greater measure. The amazing thing is that He desires to do them through you!

Yes, you read that right. The Holy Spirit will flow through common people to do uncommon feats. The Holy Spirit is the promise of the Father, which Jesus spoke of after His resurrection. He commanded His followers not to leave Jerusalem until they had received the promise of the Father. Jesus spoke of the baptism of the Holy Ghost. He was adamant when He *"commanded"* them to wait. It was not a suggestion or an option. No, it was an order. He knew that a powerless Church is ineffective. Still today, a Church with no power is inept to do the work that Jesus started and continues through the work of the Holy Spirit.

> *To whom also he shewed himself alive after his passion by many infallible proofs, being seen of them forty days, and speaking of the things pertaining to the kingdom of God: and, being assembled together with them, commanded them that they should not depart from Jerusalem, but wait for the promise of the Father, which, saith he, ye have heard of me. For John truly baptized with water; but ye shall be baptized with the Holy Ghost not many days hence* (Acts 1:3-5).

One of my greatest frustrations as a parent is when I tell one of my children to do something and they reply, "Why?" It always makes me want to give them the clichéd answer, "Because I said so!" I have discovered that most of the times when they have to ask "why" it is because they are not capable of comprehending the purpose of the instruction. For example, our church in Chattanooga is located on one of the most traveled roads in our city. My son, Gabriel, loves to run. He is so cute when he says,

"On your mark, get set, goooooooo," and then he takes off running full force. However, it was not very cute when he wanted to race in the church parking lot. When he got close to the main road, I scooped him up in my arms and said, "No, no, Gabriel." Then he proceeded to have a crying meltdown. In his eyes, I was ruining his fun. He was not capable of understanding my instruction because he is still a toddler. He could not recognize the danger of not obeying my voice. There was no way that I could sit him down and explain to him that he could be killed by a car driving at a high speed. Therefore, the answer had to be, "Because I said so." We oftentimes get frustrated when we are asking God, "Why?" But we must trust that He knows what we do not know and that His ways are higher than ours.

Why did Jesus command His followers to wait in Jerusalem for the promise of the Father?

Why couldn't the Holy Spirit have just come upon them in their houses as they went about doing their daily routines? Why did they have to wait? And why did they have to wait in Jerusalem? No doubt they didn't understand His instructions, but later they would understand when they took the promise to the streets of Jerusalem where the people had gathered for the Feast of Pentecost.

To possess the promise of God, it will often require 1) not fully understanding His commands, 2) great sacrifice, and 3) unrelenting determination. Not all are willing to pay the price.

After that, he was seen by more than 500 of his
followers at one time, most of whom are still alive,
though some have died (1 Corinthians 15:6 NLT).

The above Scripture revealed that Jesus appeared to a group of over 500, yet only 120 ended up waiting in the upper room. That is a sad statistic. That means that at least 380 did not experience this great outpouring of the Holy Spirit. Could it be because they decided not to go through the process of waiting?

Arriving there, they went into a large second-floor
room to pray. Those present were Peter, John,
Jacob, Andrew, Philip, Thomas, Bartholomew,
Matthew, Jacob (the son of Alpheus), Simon (the
zealot), Judas (the son of Jacob), and a number of
women, including Mary, Jesus' mother. His broth-
ers were there as well. All of them were united
in prayer, gripped with one passion, interceding
night and day (Acts 1:13-14 TPT).

Note the words "arriving there," meaning they obeyed the Lord's command and went to Jerusalem to wait for the promise of the Father. When they arrived in Jerusalem, only 120 of the 500 waited in the Upper Room. Look at how they waited—*"All of them were united in prayer, gripped with one passion, interceding night and day."* Those believers were not apathetic in their quest for the promise, but instead they were actively engaged in the pursuit of what Jesus spoke to them. Through their intercession, night and day, they birthed the promise. This is our model for waiting on God. So many times, as a kingdom leader, I hear individuals say, "I am just waiting on God." Most times this is a cop-out. It is a way to use spiritual language to camouflage laziness or disobedience.

There is a strength that is released in the waiting period. Personally, I do not like to wait. In fact, the biggest struggle I have is to walk in patience. And it always seems that I'm tested when I'm driving in my car. I would just love to teach a lesson to all drivers who drive in the left lane. That lesson would be that the left lane is for traffic going at an accelerated speed, and when you see my vehicle coming feel free to merge over to the slow lane. That is my flesh writing that. I have tried to explain to the Lord that patience is not necessary while I'm driving, but He didn't agree. In all seriousness, though, I have had to crucify my flesh when I am driving. I have discovered, firsthand, that patience is a requirement to possess His promise. I like to say that patience is the vehicle that faith rides in on its way to the promise.

> *For ye have need of patience, that, after ye have done the will of God, ye might receive the promise* (Hebrews 10:36).
>
> *But let patience have her perfect work, that ye may be perfect and entire, wanting nothing* (James 1:4).

One of the reasons for "the wait" is our need for patience. "Patience in the waiting" does a perfecting work in us. It brings us to the place of wanting nothing. While in the season of waiting, we usually question why God would want to delay us in receiving our promise. We often understand why He places others in a waiting season, we just can't understand why He would put us there. The verse below gives the answer to why He wants us to wait—so that we might receive an impartation of strength.

> But they that wait upon the Lord shall renew their strength; they shall mount up with wings as eagles; they shall run, and not be weary; and they shall walk, and not faint (Isaiah 40:31).

Yes, in the wait you receive an impartation of strength. Endurance is formed in you *as* you wait. Bishop T.D. Jakes one time defined *endurance* as "faith tried to its breaking point." Whenever your faith is at the breaking point, realize that you are in a test. I encourage you to endure until you pass the test! God is revealing your fortitude. You are being prepared and conditioned for what God has promised you.

> And when the day of Pentecost was fully come, they were all with one accord in one place. And suddenly there came a sound from heaven as of a rushing mighty wind, and it filled all the house where they were sitting. And there appeared unto

> *them cloven tongues like as of fire, and it sat upon each of them. And they were all filled with the Holy Ghost, and began to speak with other tongues, as the Spirit gave them utterance* (Acts 2:1-4).

I would say to you who are currently in a "waiting season" to get ready for the set time to fully come, as it did for those who waited in the upper room. The sound of wind will hit your "wait," and you too will receive a "suddenly."

> *This vision is for a future time. It describes the end, and it will be fulfilled. If it seems slow in coming, wait patiently, for it will surely take place. It will not be delayed* (Habakkuk 2:3 NLT).

The two statements *"if it seems slow in coming"* and *"it will not be delayed"* seem contradictory; however, upon closer inspection you will see that they actually complement one another. The meaning of those two statements together is an exhortation to be patient in the wait because after the wait, the suddenly will surely come. It may seem like the manifestation of the promise is taking forever while you are in the waiting period, but when you hit that "set time," His promise will come forth speedily.

Why is wind used to describe the Holy Spirit?

It is easy to perceive why "wind" is used to describe the person of the Holy Spirit. The reason is because wind cannot be seen; however, its effect on something can be seen. The Holy Spirit cannot be seen, but His affect most definitely can be. The word for *wind* in this text is the Greek word *pnoē,* meaning "the breath of life." He took a group of 120 and breathed the breath of life into them. Whenever the wind of the Holy Spirit hits a lifeless church, they are transformed into a power-filled force to forward the kingdom of God.

What was the "Holy Ghost effect" after the wind of the Holy Spirit came into the upper room?

After the 120 in the upper room encountered the "Holy Ghost effect," Peter preached with boldness. The anointing of God's power will add *super* to your *natural.* His message was not one of proclamation only, but also of demonstration.

> *Now when they saw the boldness of Peter and John, and perceived that they were unlearned and ignorant men, they marvelled; and they took knowledge of them, that they had been with Jesus* (Acts 4:13).

Did you see that? They were *"unlearned"* and considered *"ignorant,"* but their "yes" to God's assignment enabled them to be used by the Holy Spirit. Note that the religious leaders "marveled and took knowledge that they had been with Jesus."

If you want to move into the *Triple Threat Anointing*, it will require for you to have *been with Jesus.* That *secret place* with Jesus will be your lifeline to the presence of God. It is the place where you will become emptied of the flesh and refilled with the Spirit. You need to stay planted there if you want to flourish with God and do what He has called you to do.

> *But thou, when thou prayest, enter into thy closet, and when thou hast shut thy door, pray to thy Father which is in secret; and thy Father which seeth in secret shall reward thee openly* (Matthew 6:6).
>
> *He that dwelleth in the secret place of the most High shall abide under the shadow of the Almighty* (Psalm 91:1).

When I was age four, I was filled with the Holy Ghost, and it radically changed my life. Perhaps some of you are saying, "How much does a four-year-old child's life change?" For sure I wasn't out living in some sinful bondage from which He set me free, but the encounter I had with Him at age four began a hunger in me that still remains with me today at age forty-one. After that encounter with the Holy Spirit, I wanted more. I began to have nightly worship concerts for an audience of One. I would sing at the top of my lungs, giving my all in worship to Him. Do you want to know what happened? He came. Every time I would begin to worship or pray, He would come and meet with me, which increased my hunger for more of Him. It was the early years of my life that cultivated my long-lasting pursuit for more of Him. Once you really taste of Him, you cannot be satisfied with the status quo.

If you want to walk and flow in the *Triple Threat Anointing*, it has to be fueled by your intimacy with God. What I am speaking about far exceeds talent and gifting. It means walking in the authority of Heaven, being hidden in Him where you will become marked by God and chosen for His purpose. Every apostle, prophet, evangelist, pastor, teacher, and every believer must come to their secret place with God. There is *reward* that is shown openly from the *secret place*. The life and ministry of Jesus shows us the secret to flowing in the *Triple Threat Anointing*. The secret to His power is found in His daily walk with God, His lifestyle of prayer and fasting.

You need to ask the Lord for the wind of the Holy Spirit to blow upon every dead and hopeless situation in your life. Get ready to experience the *Holy Ghost effect!*

CHAPTER 11

———•○•———

THE PUSHBACK

THE COUNTERATTACK OF THE ENEMY

Whenever there is a great move of God, there is always satan's counterattack, or what I call the devil's "pushback." The enemy's desire is to stop the new move of God, and he tries to accomplish this in a plethora of ways. In this chapter, I will expose the most common methods he uses to hinder what the Lord has ordained.

Satan attempts to restrict the Church, lulling it into a type of comatose state. He doesn't mind people being Christians, as long as they live in bondage, unable to fulfill their purpose. He is not even opposed to churches being a social gathering as long as they are completely void of the power of God.

Keep in mind that satan does not have the power to create. God is the Creator. Satan can only pervert God's creation for his own use. The Bible clearly outlines the purpose of satan against us:

> *The thief cometh not, but for to **steal**, and to **kill**, and to **destroy**: I am come that they might have life, and that they might have it more abundantly* (John 10:10).

In the above Scripture verse, do you see the threefold counterattack strategy against the believer and against every move of God? Jesus narrowed down three ways that the enemy would come with the counterattack— *steal, kill,* and *destroy.* It is very interesting to me that God revealed *three* divisive strategies of the adversary against His children.

1. Jesus referred to the enemy in this Scripture as the *"thief,"* saying he would come to *"steal"* like a cunning robber, taking something that does not lawfully belong to him.

2. The next undertaking that Jesus tells us the thief would use is to *"kill."* According to Strong's Concordance, the Greek word translated *kill* is *thuo,* meaning "to blow smoke, to sacrifice, to immolate, slaughter by any purpose" and "to slay."

Jesus forewarned the Church that the enemy would try to tempt the children of God to sacrifice or give up on the promises of God. Not only would he *steal* what does not belong to him, but he also would seek to overwhelm believers with circumstances to the point they were willing to forfeit their destiny. He would kill it.

3. The third blow that the thief would try to use is *"to destroy."* If the thief has been unsuccessful at taking what lawfully belongs to another and was unable to persuade one to give up or sacrifice it by allowing it to be killed, then he will seek to destroy it. He will do his best to ruin it or pollute it, thus making it destructive instead of profitable.

   In the perspective of a move of God, this means that satan will attempt to get the leaders, as well as members of the Body of Christ, to fall into moral failure, wrong theology, or any other ways that would defile or corrupt what God is doing. The enemy is not playing games. His intention is to eradicate and stop God's purpose from being fulfilled.

Take note, Jesus warned you that if you threaten the kingdom of satan, he will try to obliterate you in three ways—*steal, kill,* and *destroy.* You are a threat to the devil when you carry the glory and release the *Triple Threat Anointing*. However, the good news is that Jesus has already destroyed the plots, plans, and schemes of the devil. He has given to the Church complete victory over every pushback attack of the devil! *"The Son of God appeared for this purpose, to destroy the works of the devil"* (1 John 3:8 AMP).

RESISTANCE FROM LEADERS OF THE LAST MOVE OF GOD

It is sad to say that one of the greatest weapons used by satan in his launch of *pushback* against believers comes through those who birthed the last move of God. He often uses those leaders to denounce the new move of God, which undermines many recipients who would benefit with the new move. Why is this? What is their motive for succumbing to satan's tactic? Some say it's from jealousy or insecurity of being "left out," or could it be simply that they have "boxed" God in, restricting Him to move exactly like they witnessed in the last move. I like to believe more optimistically of my brothers and sisters in Christ. I choose not to believe that every leader of a former move is now a "Saul" looking for their chance to kill "David."

I believe there are two different kinds of leaders from former moves of God who are used by satan to *push back* against the new movement that God is birthing:

1. Leaders who have become "burned out" with the former move of God

2. Leaders who have the same religious spirit as that of the Pharisees

Leaders Who Have Become "Burned Out" with the Former Move of God

The "burned out" leaders truly love God and His people, but they became so caught up in *working* for Him that they neglected spending time with Him, which hindered their ability to recognize that God had shifted in a new direction. Although God's desire is to partner with believers to do a mighty work on the earth, He cares more about having an intimate relationship with the individual than He does about what they can *do* for Him. I have seen these types of leaders numerous times. Sadly, these types of leaders are numerous in the Body of Christ, relying solely on their own giftings and talents instead of receiving fresh oil that comes only from spending time with Him. We have to guard ourselves from relying solely on our gifting or talents. We need Him and He desires that we want Him. I have found that this type of pushback leader is still singing the same worship songs that they sang 30 years ago. In no way am I saying that every song has to be the latest and greatest hit, for even an old hymn can be "new" when there is a fresh wind of the Holy Spirit blowing upon it. There should be no room for repetitious monotonous rituals in our church services. God is a progressive God. That is not to say that He, Himself, changes or His message of truth changes. Those two things will never change! His methods, though, do change, as well as His seasons.

Are you ready for God's seasons to change? I currently reside in Chattanooga, Tennessee. Our weather, for the most part, is what one would expect in relation to all of the four seasons of winter, summer, spring, and fall. Chattanooga is neither Chicago, where the temperature drops into the negatives when it is winter, nor is it Florida, where the temperatures can drop lower than normal but usually not to the point of freezing.

Even now, as I write this chapter, a cold front has moved into our region. Yesterday, we had a high of 73 degrees. It felt great outside. It was beautiful. I even commented to my wife that I would love for it to stay just like this for the rest of the year. But overnight in a matter of hours, the temperature dropped—the high today was 32 degrees. There was a sudden shift of seasons. Yet I was prepared for the turn in weather. I prepared in advance for the cold temperatures. My point is this— God has times and seasons. We cannot allow ourselves to be unprepared for God's next season. We must walk in synchronization with Heaven's agenda.

Have you ever noticed "that person" who is not dressed appropriately for the season? To me it always seems to be a teenage guy wearing shorts in the middle of winter. It's as if he is playing a game of *Can I make through the winter wearing my shorts without getting frostbitten?* I want to say to him, "Why are you not dressed for this time of the year? Do you not feel the cold wind piercing through you? Why do you feel the need to be rebellious against the weather?"

On the other hand, worse is the person who insists on wearing their winter coat and sweater when it is hot outside, simply because they like the way they look in it. I am always concerned they will pass out or have a heat stroke. The season has shifted and they are either unwilling, unable, or simply don't care to change with it. This is exactly what I see in the spirit with many leaders, as well as some believers. They are either unwilling, unable, or simply don't care to change with God's new season.

When Jesus taught His disciples a model for prayer referred to as *The Lord's Prayer,* He instructed them to ask the Father, *"Give us day by day our daily bread"* (Luke 11:3). Jesus was conveying a larger truth than just asking for our daily necessities. He used it to express a much grander concept. The meaning of the word *bread* is that He used it as a metaphor for revelation and salvation. *"But he answered and said, It is written, Man shall not live by bread alone, but by every word that proceedeth out of the mouth of God"* (Matt. 4:4). Did you see that? While being tempted by the devil, Jesus stated that we do not live by natural bread alone *but by every word that proceeds out of the mouth of God.* We do not live only by natural food but by the supernatural words of God. The revelations that we gain from the words that come from the mouth of God are bread for us to sustain supernatural life.

God never intended for us to feast today on yesterday's revelation. He has fresh bread (revelation) for us. I get alarmed when ministers preach the exact same message with all the same jokes, points, and delivery that they preached 20 years ago. Where is the fresh bread? I am not saying that ministers should not use the same text or tell the same story. My church could tell you that I sometimes minister from the same scriptural text; when I do, there's always a fresh wind to it. It's time for us to stop feasting on stale bread and get unstuck by going into our prayer room to receive fresh bread.

Leaders Who Have the Same Religious Spirit as That of the Pharisees

The leaders with the religious spirit are terrified of losing their positions of power. They don't want something fresh from God because it would challenge them to change. These leaders have a *business as usual* mindset. They do not want the Holy Spirit to disturb what they are doing. They are happy and content with going through religious ritual. They have closed the door to the Spirit of God.

This is the leader or church that prefers production to the presence of God, professionalism over power, and pleasing people above pleasing God. When this leader begins to care more about what the people think about them than what the Lord thinks about them, then comes the fall.

King Saul was anointed to be king. God used him, and he won great victories for God's people. Slowly, King Saul's priorities and his view of himself began to change. Pride crept in and he was deceived to believe that it had become about him. He wanted the people's admiration over God's. The praise of man can never compete with the approval of Heaven. Man is a cheap substitute for God.

> *And Samuel said to Saul, Thou hast done foolishly: thou hast not kept the commandment of the Lord thy God, which he commanded thee: for now would the Lord have established thy kingdom upon Israel for ever. But now thy kingdom shall not continue: the Lord hath sought him a man after his own heart, and the Lord hath commanded him to be captain over his people, because thou hast not kept that which the Lord commanded thee* (1 Samuel 13:13-14).

Saul's reign as king of Israel is a lesson for every leader. Stay small in your own eyes and allow God to be magnified. Don't allow the fact that God uses you to puff up your pride and swell up your ego. If we do not want to be those leaders who push back against how God is moving, then we must remain confidently humble. Our confidence should be in Jesus and His desire to use us. Humility is not going to the extreme where you have low self-esteem and cannot receive a compliment. I have found that people who cannot receive a compliment or praise in any manner are really operating in false humility, which is a form of pride. We must walk in balance and be in step with the Holy Spirit in every area of our life.

DELAY

I heard the Lord say to His people, *"Playtime is over!"* The enemy has a strategic purpose to overwhelm God's people with delay and move them out of position. Satan's desire is to stop you from doing what God has called you to do. He does not want the *Triple Threat Anointing* to flow through God's people. Why? The answer is quite simple—it is a threat to hell!

Delay is often the tactic the enemy uses to force God's people to get out of combat and on the playground. We see this is what happened with the children of Israel when Moses delayed in coming down from the mountain after meeting with God.

> *And when the people saw that Moses delayed to come down out of the mount, the people gathered themselves together unto Aaron, and said unto him, Up, make us gods, which shall go before us; for as for this Moses, the man that brought us*

*up out of the land of Egypt, we wot not what is
become of him. And Aaron said unto them, Break
off the golden earrings, which are in the ears of
your wives, of your sons, and of your daughters,
and bring them unto me. And all the people brake
off the golden earrings which were in their ears,
and brought them unto Aaron. And he received
them at their hand, and fashioned it with a
graving tool, after he had made it a molten calf:
and they said, These be thy gods, O Israel, which
brought thee up out of the land of Egypt* (Exodus
32:1-4).

Whenever we face delay, we become tempted to take
things into our own hands. Delay caused God's people to
take the spoils of the Egyptians (their blessings from God)
and throw them into the fire to make a man-made idol
of gold, molded into the image of a calf. It was a replica
of Apis, the bull that was worshiped back in Egypt. Did
you get that? Because of the delay of Moses, the children
of Israel were ready to forsake the God who had brought
them out of Egypt and parted the Red Sea in favor of a
replica of the god of the Egyptians. They had lost their
mandate and in turn settled for what was familiar.

We are all faced with delay on our way to our land
of promise. In the time of waiting you should be on
guard and refuse to settle for less than the inheritance
that God has promised to you. There is no time to waste.

God is calling loud and clear: *"All hands on deck. Get in line. Stay in line. The time is now. Souls are hanging in the balance."*

> *And all the people brake off the golden earrings which were in their ears, and brought them unto Aaron. And he received them at their hand, and fashioned it with a graving tool, after he had made it a molten calf: and they said, These be thy gods, O Israel, which brought thee up out of the land of Egypt. And when Aaron saw it, he built an altar before it; and Aaron made proclamation, and said, To morrow is a feast to the Lord* (Exodus 32:3-5).

Look at what the Israelites did while Moses was delayed. They made a golden calf and declared that it was their god. In Verse 4, the Hebrew word translated *gods* is the name *Elohim.* And in Verse 5, the Hebrew word translated *Lord* is the name *Jehovah.* Not only did they make a golden idol of their earrings and jewelry, but they also gave it the credit for their miraculous deliverance from Egypt and ascribed to it the names of God. How blinded they had become, just because they believed they were inconveniently or unjustly delayed.

What did the people do when they received an idol to replace their God? The Bible says, *"and the people sat down to eat and to drink, and rose up to play"* (Exod. 32:6). Take note of the words used to describe the people's actions: "They rose up to play." God is saying to us, *"Playtime is over! I am doing a new thing that will be marked by My glory. Do not allow delay to cause you to step out of alignment and to play with the enemy's distractions."*

> *But they that wait upon the Lord shall renew their strength; they shall mount up with wings as eagles; they shall run, and not be weary; and they shall walk, and not faint* (Isaiah 40:31).

There is strength in one's "wait." Most people deem waiting a frustration or an obstruction to get to where they are going. However, this is not the type of "wait" that the prophet described would "renew their strength." Much to the contrary, the word *wait* here means to hope for and anticipate. I use the analogy of a waiter or server to describe what it means to wait. They are doing something! They are active! Often I hear people say things like, "I'm just waiting on the Lord." What they are actually doing is nothing! They are excusing themselves to be lazy! God desires that we "wait" by actively pursuing after His will. When they "waited" in Jerusalem for the promise of the Father, which was the Holy Ghost, they were active in prayer. They were anticipating, hoping for, and fully expecting that God would fulfill His promise to them.

It is time for you to arise—not to play but to shine with His glory. It is your season to arise in the *Triple Threat Anointing*, empowering you to change your generation:

"Arise, shine; for thy light is come, and the glory of the Lord is risen upon thee" (Isa. 60:1). You have been chosen to be a carrier of His glory. He desires to manifest His glory through you. The same Spirit that raised Christ from the dead now lives and dwells inside of you.

The goal of this chapter is in no way to glorify the enemy, but rather to expose him and make sure that he does not take advantage of you—*"lest Satan should take advantage of us: for we are not ignorant of his devices"* (2 Cor. 2:11). Satan and demonic spirits are very real and they are actively engaged to oppose God's plan for your life, your family, your city, and your generation. Nevertheless, always remember that Jesus defeated satan and his kingdom by paying the price of redemption on the cross. Jesus literally stripped the weaponry of the enemy, leaving him totally bare and exposed!

> *And having spoiled principalities and powers, he made a shew of them openly, triumphing over them in it* (Colossians 2:15).

In the above Scripture verse, the Greek word *apekdyomai* is translated as *spoiled,* meaning to "to strip off clothes or arms" and to "despoil, disarm." To me, *The Passion Translation* translates what Jesus did for us the best:

> *Then Jesus made a public spectacle of all the powers and principalities of darkness, stripping away from them every weapon and all their*

spiritual authority and power to accuse us. And by the power of the cross, Jesus led them around as prisoners in a procession of triumph. He was not their prisoner; they were his! (Colossians 2:15 TPT)

The imagery of the Scripture above paints an extremely vivid picture of Jesus having stripped the enemy of his authority over the redeemed of Christ. It reveals the procession of Christ's triumph that took place as Jesus led forth principalities, powers, and rulers of darkness, stripped bare as a spectacle before all of Heaven. I don't think our human minds can conceive or have the words to articulate the magnitude of the victory that was won for us.

CHAPTER 12

SUSTAINING THE TRIPLE THREAT ANOINTING

A LIFESTYLE OF PRAYER AND FASTING

And one of the multitude answered and said, Master, I have brought unto thee my son, which hath a dumb [mute] spirit; And wheresoever he taketh him, he teareth him: and he foameth, and gnasheth with his teeth, and pineth away: and I spake to thy disciples that they should cast him out; and they could not. He answereth him, and saith, O faithless generation, how long shall I be with you? how long shall I suffer you? bring him unto me. And they brought him unto him: and when he saw him, straightway the spirit tare him; and he fell on the ground, and wallowed foaming. And he asked his father, How long is it ago since this came unto him? And he said, Of a child. And ofttimes it hath cast him into the fire, and into the waters, to destroy him: but if thou canst do any thing, have compassion on us, and help us. Jesus said unto him, If thou canst believe, all things are possible to him that believeth. And straightway the father of the child cried out, and said with tears, Lord, I believe; help thou mine unbelief. When Jesus saw that the people came running together, he rebuked the foul spirit, saying unto him, Thou dumb [mute] *and deaf spirit, I charge thee, come out of him, and enter no more into him. And the spirit cried, and rent* [tore] *him sore* [throwing him into a terrible convulsion], *and came out of him: and he was as one dead; insomuch that many said, He is dead. But Jesus took him by the hand, and lifted him up; and he arose. And when he was come into the house, his disciples asked him privately, Why could not we cast him out? And he said unto them, This kind can come forth by nothing, but by prayer and fasting* (Mark 9:17-29).

This story is the perfect example of the power of God being demonstrated by a lifestyle of prayer and fasting. A father brought his son to the disciples, being desperate for God to do something for him. The plan of the enemy was clear—it was to destroy this boy. The enemy's objective is always to *steal, kill,* and *destroy.* The demonic spirits would cause physical malaises in the boy. He not only had a "deaf and mute spirit," but he also had a "lunatic spirit." The word *lunatic* is translated from the Greek word *seleiazomai,* which means "moonstruck." It was their belief at the time that epilepsy was caused by the full moon, because the attacks were worse at these times. However, we know that they were caused by a demonic spirit. This boy was completely controlled by demons.

The lunatic spirit would cause the boy epileptic episodes where he would fall to the ground in convulsions. It caused him to foam at the mouth and his teeth would gnash together uncontrollably. The demonic spirits would cause him to fall into the fire and also into water, trying to destroy him. His parents were at their wits' end. They did not know what to do for him. Completely out of answers, they brought him to the disciples, hoping they could help him. They could not. Like so many today, they were void of the power of God. At this point, Jesus stepped in and rebuked the disciples for their lack of faith. He said, "Bring him to Me." As they were bringing the boy to Jesus, the spirit caused the boy to fall to the ground, wallowing and foaming from his mouth.

Jesus asked the father of the boy, "How long has he been like this?" The father replied, "Since he was a child." In the Gospel of Luke, it says that Jesus rebuked the unclean spirit out of this boy. *Unclean* is described as "lewd, impure, unchaste, obscene, lustful, participating in unlawful sexual behavior." From this definition of "unclean" we can conclude that possession of the boy came through some sort of sexual perversion. This is how the enemy gained access into his life. Jesus rebuked the "foul spirit" and commanded it to come out of the boy and forbade it to enter into him again.

When I first became a pastor, I had a couple in my church and the husband had a problem with lust and drugs. He had a job that required him to travel, but they were still faithful in their church attendance. The wife would pressure him to meet with me, asking me to pray for his deliverance. I would pray for him and rebuke demonic spirits and command them to go. He would be delivered. His whole countenance would change, but I began to notice a pattern. At least once every two months, *she* was bringing him to me. The Lord revealed to me that when he would travel for his job he would have sexual activity with prostitutes. I asked him about this and he denied it. A few months later, he was arrested with a prostitute. The wife was brokenhearted, as you can well imagine; again, she asked me to help him get delivered. I rebuked the devil and the demonic spirit left his body and I told them both that he had to make the decision to remain free. There would have to be a change in his habits and behavior in order to stay free.

When the wife came to me the next time asking me to please pray for her husband, I heard the Holy Spirit speak to me. He warned me not to pray for him because he was not ready to be free. I told her, "I cannot pray for your husband. I would be doing you and him a disservice because he does not yet desire to be totally free. Every time he is delivered and then picks it back up, it comes back seven times stronger. I do both you and him a disservice."

When the unclean spirit is gone out of a man, he walketh through dry places, seeking rest, and findeth none. Then he saith, I will return into my house from whence I came out; and when he is come, he findeth it empty, swept, and garnished. Then goeth he, and taketh with himself seven other spirits more wicked than himself, and they enter in and dwell there: and the last state of that man is worse than the first. Even so shall it be also unto this wicked generation (Matthew 12:43-45).

When Jesus had cast out the demon from the epileptic boy, the disciples asked Him a question. His answer to them revealed the secret to dealing with the devil.

And when he was come into the house, his disciples asked him privately, Why could not we cast him out? And he said unto them, This kind can

come forth by nothing, but by prayer and fasting
(Mark 9:28-29).

Prayer and fasting were not just something He did at the first of the year or when He needed an answer about something in particular. It was a discipline that He lived. He was crucifying His flesh long before He ever went to the cross. If we, too, desire to walk in this power, we must live a laid-down life of prayer and fasting.

One day Jesus was praying in a certain place. When he finished, one of his disciples said to him, "Lord, teach us to pray, just as John taught his disciples" (Luke 11:1 NIV).

Very revealing here is that the disciples wanted to be taught to pray. They wanted to learn how to pray like Jesus. They could have asked Him anything, but that which interested them was His life of power, and they recognized that it came through prayer. They saw Him walking in victory. They saw Him performing the mighty works of God. I wonder how many Christians there are today who want to take the time to learn to pray? Sadly, I believe the majority of Christians would ask questions like, "What are the five steps to my break-through? Or how do I access favor on my life? Or can you show me the principles to become wealthy?" (All of the above questions are already answered in the Bible.) We must first learn to pray if we desire to do the "greater works than Jesus" that were promised to us.

Verily, verily, I say unto you, He that believeth on me, the works that I do shall he do also; and greater works than these shall he do; because I go unto my Father (John 14:12).

When God gave me the dream of this soon-coming move of God and then later revealed to me the principles of the *Triple Threat Anointing*, He had you in mind. In fact, it is not by mere coincidence that you have read this book. No, it was by divine appointment. God is inviting you to step into another dimension of His power and for you to experience firsthand the same anointing in which Jesus walked. This movement will be birthed by those who are carrying the weighty glory and armed with the *Triple Threat*.

Thank you for taking the time to read this book. I pray that it has sparked a fire within you and that it has stirred hunger inside you to not only see this next move of God but to play an active role in it. The Lord is looking for those who will lay down their lives and pick up the mantle of the *Triple Threat Anointing* to birth a movement of His glory that will change this generation. If the world has ever needed a genuine awakening, it is today. God is calling you to be an agent of awakening.

I encourage you to pray the following prayer and mean it with all your heart:

Father, I pray for You to release the Triple Threat Anointing in my life and to fill me to overflowing. I ask You to send me forth as an agent of change in my family, my city, my nation, and to this generation. Empower me to do the "greater works" that are promised in Your Word. I sincerely desire for You to activate the supernatural power of Your Spirit within me. My heart's desire is to be used of You and for my life to give You glory. I realize that I am not here to live an average, run-of-the-mill life, for I am an ambassador of the kingdom of Heaven. I am a child of the Most High God. I will flow in the supernatural anointing of salvation, healing, and deliverance. I ask this in the Name of Jesus.

ABOUT ANDREW TOWE

Andrew Towe is an emerging prophetic voice to this generation! He and his wife, Brooke, are the lead pastors of Ramp Church Chattanooga. Andrew is also a sought-after conference speaker and itinerant minister. He actively demonstrates God's power by flowing in the gifts of the Spirit and prophetically declaring the Word of God. Andrew has been featured on many leading broadcasts including Sid Roth's *It's Supernatural!,* Trinity Broadcasting Network, and Christian Television Network. He is a regular contributing writer for *Charisma Magazine* and *The Elijah List.* His mandate is to ignite the fires of global revival and awakening. Andrew's ministry is also very active through social media and his website.

Andrew Towe Ministries	**Ramp Church Chattanooga**
P.O. Box 888	3975 Brainerd Road
Chattanooga, TN 37414	Chattanooga, Tn 37411
andrewtowe.org	ramp.church/chatt
Facebook:	**Facebook:**
Andrew Towe	Ramp Church Chattanooga
Instagram:	**Instagram:**
Andrew Towe	rampchurchchattanooga